Ready,
Set,
Grow

A 52 WEEK
DEVOTIONAL FOR TEENS

Hannah Beth Brown

THIS BOOK IS DEDICATED TO:

MY ZOO CREW

Mom – the nuts and seeds lady who lives in leggings and masters a head stand

Dad – the running, hummer, Mr. Fix-It, math tutor who is the glue to the zoo crew

Mary Claire – the decisive, dancing queen with more new phases than the moon

Noah – the bike riding, drone flying, backpacking weatherman in khaki shorts

Muntu – the food lover, Taekwondo master with the strength to move a piano all by himself

TABLE OF CONTENTS

There's a phrase I hear people saying right now that always causes me great alarm: "I just have to be true to myself." While I get the fact that each of us has feelings and we don't want to live in denial of what's affecting us, I also know that hurt feelings don't often want to cooperate with holy instructions. In other words, if I'm wanting to be true to myself, I must make sure I'm being true to my most healed, surrendered to God self, or my choices could be disastrous. Just because something "feels" good, doesn't mean it is good. Just because something feels "right" doesn't mean it is right.

There's got to be a better source guiding me and my choices than my own feelings. Feelings are good indicators that something needs to be addressed in my life, but should never be dictators of how I act and react. It's God's word that should guide me into all truth each and every day. As John 8:32 teaches, it's the truth that sets us free.

But as we look closely at this incredible verse promising freedom, we get a deeper understanding of what we must do to walk in that promise each day. John 8:31-32: "Jesus said, If you hold to my teaching, you are really my disciples. Then you will know the truth, and the truth will set you free." It is crucial that we hold onto Jesus's teaching every day and factor His truth into our perspectives, our choices, and how we treat other people. So, instead of saying we are being true to ourselves to justify acting how we feel, a much healthier statement would be, "I just have to be true to God's word."

That's why I'm so delighted by this devotional book by Hannah Beth Brown. Though the book is filled with personal stories and insights, the point of every entry is to connect us to God's word. As we see Hannah Beth making those connections between what God's word teaches and the experiences of her everyday life, we can start to do the same. She so beautifully models what it means to weave God's word into each experience we have and to intentionally look for evidence of God's incredible presence all around us.

As you use this devotional each day, I pray that more and more, like Hannah Beth, you'll start to recognize God's hand of activity all around you. Never have we needed this reminder more than right now. Never have we needed to be more true to God's word and less consumed and controlled by our own feelings than right now. When this world is in constant turmoil, tensions between people so high, and everything from politics to economics feel so very uncertain, we truly can have a peace that stabilizes us and comforts us. This is the peace that God promises for those who build their lives on the solid foundation of His Truth.

– Lysa Terkeurst, *Author and President of Proverbs 31 Ministries*

INTRODUCTION

"Ready, Set, Grow" was designed for YOU! This book includes fifty-two weekly devotionals to help you learn more about Christ. Each devotional is composed of three main parts: "Ready," "Set," and "Grow."

READY

"READY" is defined as, "to prepare someone or something for an activity or purpose." This section of the devotional includes a personal story and message that should prepare you to absorb His truths and act upon them.

SET

"SET" is defined as "to put, lay, or stand something in a specified place or position." This portion of the devotion contains multiple scripture verses. Scripture allows us to understand God's story and our position as His most treasured and beloved children.

GROW

"GROW" is "to progress to maturity." The last portion of each devotion includes a personal challenge or activity that is intended to mature your faith through intentional actions.

I chose to write a devotion that was weekly rather than daily for a very important reason. My prayer is that you would marinate on the contents of each devotion all week, reflecting on the story, memorizing the scriptures, and engaging in the suggested activities. Colossians 2:6-7 says, "Therefore, as you received Christ Jesus the Lord, so walk in him, rooted and built up in him and established in the faith, just as you were taught, abounding in thanksgiving."

My only goal in writing "Ready, Set, Grow" is to magnify the name of Christ. My prayer is that this book would allow you to draw nearer to Christ and learn more of His magnificent character and unending love. 1 Corinthians 2:9 says, "No eye has seen, no ear has heard, and no mind has imagined what God has prepared for those who love Him."

God has big plans for you, so without further ado, Ready...Set...Grow!

READY

Have you ever made anything using clay?

I remember making a few clay projects in 3rd grade art class. At the time, I was so proud of how amazing I thought they were, but looking at them now, I must admit… they look absolutely terrible. I find it interesting that the Bible talks about clay. Many of you may be familiar with the phrase, "God is the potter, and we are the clay" (Isaiah 64:8). It was not until I heard a sermon about this verse that I studied it on my own and began to better understand its meaning. God is telling us that He is our Creator. He is holding us in His hands and lovingly shaping us.

Imagine the potter grabbing a large amount of clay to use for his work. Now, pause for a quick second and picture what clay looks like. It is not very pretty, but afterward, once the shape is formed, fired, painted, and polished, it becomes something beautiful. It is such a dramatic transformation that it is hard to believe that dry, dull clay becomes a shiny, beautiful creation. In the same way, God transforms sinners like us into His masterpieces. We start out as clay, which represents our lives before we accept Jesus into our hearts. When we accept Jesus as our true Lord and Savior, He begins to mold and shape us into who He has created us to be for His glory. In this stage, the potter usually folds, pinches, and rubs the clay to change its appearance. Likewise, the Lord makes changes within our lives. Some examples include adding new friends, eliminating poor influences, and reshaping habits. It is through these changes that God molds us into His masterpieces.

One of the most important steps for making durable pottery is the heating process. Firing the pottery allows the weak clay to become hard and durable; therefore, after heating, the clay is much more useful. The heat changes the clay by removing trapped water and other imperfections, leaving it stronger. Similarly, life's hurts, pains, and trials are used by God to make us stronger.

Genesis 2:7 tells us that God created man from the very dust of the earth. The Master Potter can make beauty from ashes. When it comes to people, God only has the "messy things" to work with. None of us are perfect, we all have made mistakes, and we all continue to sin; therefore, we are covered in "dirt." However, Jesus's blood washes us so we can become clean. God knows we are not perfect, and He uses our flaws to shape us. The Lord is then able to transform us into His amazing masterpieces.

SET

"O house of Israel, can I not do with you as this potter has done? declares the Lord. Behold, like the clay in the potter's hand, so are you in my hand, O house of Israel."
Jeremiah 18:6

"For we are his workmanship, created in Christ Jesus for good works, which God prepared beforehand, that we should walk in them."
Ephesians 2:10

"So God created man in his own image, in the image of God he created him; male and female he created them."
Genesis 1:27

GROW

God is our Creator, and He can make anyone beautiful, not for our glory, but for His. He has prepared each of us to do amazing things to advance the Kingdom. Let the Lord shape and mold you into His perfect creation. This will allow others to see the power of God through your transformation. What characteristic about yourself do you think God would want to reshape or mold? I challenge you this week to memorize Jeremiah 18:6 and write it in the space below. Read all these verses and study them. Ask the Lord to open your heart and mind to receive the truth from His Word.

READY

In a culture of rushing and running, we end up having to "work Jesus into our schedule." With school from morning to afternoon, extracurricular activities from afternoon to evening, and homework to infinity and beyond, we are busy people living busy lives! We are always jumping from one activity to the next which makes intentional time with Jesus difficult to squeeze into our schedules. However, if Jesus is the most important part of our lives, we must prioritize Him – and our time with Him – above all. He must come before academic excellence, before athletic performance, and before everything else in our lives that calls for our time and attention. It may be hard to find time for Jesus. You may not feel like spending time with Him, but taking time out of your day for Him will CHANGE YOUR LIFE!

On a typical morning, I wake up, get ready for school, and have my devotion time. Originally, my quiet time seemed brief – averaging about ten minutes. Over time, it increased from ten minutes to thirty minutes to an hour. Because of the extra time I had during the COVID-19 pandemic, I was able to spend even more time each day with the Lord. Thirty minutes or an hour may seem like forever to some people, but you can start with just five minutes. The key is that you block out time specifically to spend with Jesus. During this time, put away your phone, go somewhere quiet, and prepare your heart to receive whatever He has for you that day. This is time for you to connect with God, so it should only be you and Him.

Because everyone's relationship with God is
personal, this time will look different depending on the
person. Some people may prefer reading their Bible in the quiet
intimacy of their room; others prefer walking outside in the Lord's
beautiful creation; some may like listening to praise music or a
sermon. It is such a gift that there are so many different ways to spend
time with God!

Why do you need to set aside time for God? Because He created you,
and He knows you better than anyone else in the world. God knows
more about you than your parents, siblings, and even your best friend

(and best friends know a lot!). Jesus desires for you to come to Him because He loves you and wants to spend time with you. If you want to live a Christ-centered life, start by slowing down and setting aside time for Jesus. He cannot communicate how He intends to set you apart unless you set apart time for Him.

SET

"But seek first the kingdom of God and his righteousness, and all these things will be added to you."

Matthew 6:33

"Be still and know that I am God."

Psalms 46:10

GROW

This week spend at least ten minutes each day with Jesus. This could be praying, reading the Word, or simply resting in His presence. This is the only way He can begin to set you apart for His Kingdom. Journal the distractions in your life that keep you from Him. Write down changes you noticed throughout the week as you set aside time for just Jesus.

READY

I had the privilege to travel to Honduras on a mission trip with the church I attended when I lived in Baton Rouge, Louisiana. The very first night we were there, my mom and I woke up at 2:00 A.M. to a loud rooster crowing. We were completely exhausted from a long day of traveling. We waited a few minutes, hoping and praying that the rooster would calm down or at least get a little quieter so we could continue our much-needed rest. The rooster never stopped crowing at all, not even a little bit! All night the rooster crowed and crowed. Just when we thought there was hope it was going to stop, the rooster started back up again. This occurred every single night while we were there, and it drove us absolutely crazy! Unlike all the other rooms, our room did not have a fan to block out the noise. I have never thought violent things about any animal… until I encountered this evil rooster. I was tempted to chop its head off in the middle of the night!

Just like this rooster, the devil can get on your nerves! In fact, he does anything and everything he can to annoy you. For example, the devil uses doubt, anxiety, and comparison to mess with your mind. Do not be discouraged though, because in Ephesians 6, God tells us exactly how to handle the enemy by giving us specific instructions on how to face his evil schemes. If we want to defeat the devil, we must do it through Christ and the armor He gives us. God says that with this armor on, we will be able to withstand evil and stand firm. The Lord says that we must wear the belt of truth, the breastplate of righteousness, the shoes of peace, the shield of faith, the

helmet of salvation, and the sword of the spirit. God is not being literal with these wardrobe choices; He is making spiritual references. First, the belt of truth symbolizes the protection God's word provides us from Satan's lies. Next, the breastplate of righteousness protects our hearts, which are most vulnerable to Satan's attacks because our emotions and self-worth are stored here. The shoes of peace represent protection from Satan's attempts to persuade us that spreading the Gospel is a waste of time. The armor will help us fight all battles so that we can be prepared for whatever comes our way. God reminds us to be prepared and ready to share the Good News with others so that they too may be saved one day by Christ. The shield of faith protects us from the devil's fiery arrows of temptations and setbacks and reminds us to cling to our hope in Christ. The helmet of salvation provides safety over our minds from doubts Satan may place in our lives. Lastly, the sword of the Spirit protects us from doubt and helps us trust in the Word of God. The devil does his best to tempt us and make us question God, but God is bigger than anything Satan could ever use to harm us. Do not let the devil get under your skin like that rooster. Have confidence in the Lord and His Word, and face your battles knowing that He is with you and has given you the armor you need to take on the roosters in your life!

SET

"Finally, be strong in the Lord and in the strength of his might. Put on the whole armor of God, that you may be able to stand against the schemes of the devil. For we do not wrestle against flesh and blood, but against the rulers, against the authorities, against the cosmic powers over this present darkness, against the spiritual forces of evil in the heavenly places. Therefore take up the whole armor of God, that you may be able to withstand in the evil day, and having done all, to stand firm. Stand therefore, having fastened on the belt of truth, and having put on the breastplate of righteousness, and, as shoes for your feet, having put on the readiness given by the gospel of peace. In all circumstances take up the shield of faith, with which you can extinguish all the flaming darts of the evil one; and take the helmet of salvation, and the sword of the Spirit, which is the word of God." Ephesians 6:10-17

GROW

The next time you are faced with a difficult challenge or temptation, pray asking for God's strength, wisdom, guidance, and armor. Also, I encourage you to draw out a picture of what you think the armor of Christ would look like. Do not worry if you are not an artist; I am not either!

READY

On New Year's morning, my mom and dad decided to make a special breakfast for our family and friends who were visiting us over the holidays. We all sat down at the table with our plates full of pancakes, bacon, and fruit. We were all very hungry and quickly began to eat. Soon after, my mom exclaimed, "These pancakes taste terrible! Is it just me or does anyone else taste that, too?" Everyone hesitantly agreed that the pancakes did have an unusual taste, but no one wanted to hurt my parents' feelings. My dad recalled that he used the deluxe version of the pancake recipe which called for some extra flavor-enhancing ingredients, one being sugar. Then, he realized that instead of adding sugar into the bowl, he accidentally poured in salt! Both ingredients were stored in clear, unlabeled containers, leading to a predictable mix-up. Even though the recipe did not require a huge amount of sugar, the flavor from the salt my dad added quickly spread throughout the entire batter. One of our friends said, "When I bit into my pancake, it tasted like it was dipped in the ocean." Since none of us could bear to finish the rest of our salty pancakes, my mom made an entire new batch. The salty ones went straight into the trash can, and we all had a good laugh!

Today, salt is primarily used as an ingredient in many recipes. However, in Biblical times it served a variety of other purposes. In fact, in those times it was very valuable and was used as a method of payment for Roman soldiers. It was also required

by God in some of the Old Testament sacrifices. Salt was
(and still is) used as a preservative. Salt added to meats and fish allows
them to be saved for later by killing any microbial growth that could
cause them to go bad. It was (and still is) used as a flavor enhancer.
If you take bland, flavorless food and add just the right amount of
salt (not the amount in our "ocean-dipped" pancakes), it gives a very
pleasing flavor. Like salt, we should be an enhancer of God's love to
others. God tells us to be "the salt and the light," meaning that we
are called to share His love with others. This is a high calling because

it requires us to reflect Christ's love. Just as the small amount of salt in our pancake batter produced a strong flavor, you can serve as the small, special ingredient to make a big difference in someone else's life.

SET

"You are the salt of the earth, but if salt has lost its taste, how shall its saltiness be restored? It is no longer good for anything except to be thrown out and trampled under people's feet. You are the light of the world. A city set on a hill cannot be hidden. Nor do people light a lamp and put it under a basket, but on a stand, and it gives light to all in the house. In the same way, let your light shine before others, so that they may see your good works and give glory to your Father who is in heaven."

Matthew 5:13-16

GROW

I challenge you to read Matthew 5:13-16 every day this week. This verse has beautiful imagery. Have fun this week illustrating these verses below. I chose to draw the city on the hilltop. What will you draw?

READY

During the summer before my eighth-grade school year, my friend's mom convinced me to run cross-country with her daughter. I had never run before, but to my surprise, I loved it! When the idea was first proposed, I thought it was crazy. In fact, the first couple of times I ran, I actually did NOT enjoy it. I remember at the team tryouts I thought I was going to die ... literally. We had to run a mile loop twice in under twenty minutes. I did make it to the finish line, but not without lots of heavy breathing, sweating, and maybe a few stops to "tie my shoes" (which was really an opportunity to catch my breath). For sure, it was difficult. However, the more I ran, the more natural it felt, and the easier it became. Now, running is my favorite activity.

Sometimes, God's plan for us is unexpected. This unexpectedness comes from our plans and God's plans contradicting one another. I would have never, ever thought about running cross-country, but God knew what was best for me and used my friend's mom to help me see His plan. My cross-country experience parallels our lives as Christians. Many of us have a plan formed in our minds about our future. We predict what the future will be from our view, but God sees the entire picture. He sometimes calls us to do things we do not expect. For example, I was a dancer from the age of three to fifteen. I never expected I would stop dancing and commit to running. Trust that God's plan is always better than yours. His ways are higher than our ways. At first, I did not know why God called me to run; however, now, I see that He had a plan all along.

The unexpected is not always enjoyable or exciting, but I challenge you to persevere. Running was not something I looked forward to at first, but God has used running to stretch, challenge, and grow my faith. When the unexpected comes your way, embrace it and know that God will give you the strength you need. There is nothing too hard for Him. Let God lead your life because He knows you best and sees the entire picture in the frame. Inky Johnson, a former football player, said, "When you are in the picture, you are unable to see it in its entirety," but God can see everything and desires the best for you, even if it is different than your plan.

"For I know the plans I have for you, declares the Lord, plans for welfare and not for evil, to give you a future and a hope."

Jeremiah 29:11

"Many are the plans in the mind of a man, but it is the purpose of the Lord that will stand."

Proverbs 19:21

"For my thoughts are not your thoughts, neither are your ways my ways, declares the Lord. For as the heavens are higher than the earth, so are my ways higher than your ways and my thoughts than your thoughts."

Isaiah 55: 8-9

GROW

Is there something unexpected God is calling you toward? If so, answer Him with obedience, and trust in His plans for you. Where do you see yourself in five, ten, and fifteen years? Remember these plans are yours, not God's. Always trust His plans. Journal your thoughts below, and then give God control of your future by allowing Him to do the unexpected in your life. Remember, God's ways are higher than our ways! He knows what is best and sees the entire picture!

READY

Four years ago, my family adopted my brother, Muntu, from the Democratic Republic of the Congo (DRC) in Africa. I was eleven years old when my family began the adoption process, and I had no idea it involved so much time, commitment, and money. Do not even get me started on all the paperwork my parents had to complete! We were matched with Muntu when he was five years old; however, he was not able to come to America until he was eight years old. A key reason for the delay was that the DRC closed its international adoption program, preventing adopted children from leaving the country until the DRC reopened its program. This was extremely disappointing for our family. We were so close to the final stage of adoption! Their doors remained closed for several years, and many people began to question if our adoption would be completed. The process was hard because we did not know how long we would be waiting. However, through this situation, God taught me a lot about patience.

Many people agree that patience is one of the hardest fruits of the Spirit to live out. God works in our lives but does so on His timeline and not ours. He is faithful to follow through on His promises, but the timing may be different than we envision. God never promised that we would get Muntu quickly, but only that he would become a part of our family. Waiting requires patience that does not come *from us*; it comes from God's Spirit living *in us*. No one likes to wait, but God shows us in His Word and in our own lives that His promises

are worth the wait. It is almost
like waiting in a line at Disney World. No one enjoys waiting in the
long line of people, moving inches per minute, and staring at the
sign that says "1 hour wait" for what feels like forever. Yet, when you
finally arrive at the front of the line, the experience is worth the wait.
Not only is waiting worth it, God rewards those who patiently wait
on Him. In fact, reflecting on waiting for Muntu to arrive in America,
I believe that the timing was perfect. The Lord knew the exact time

for all six of us to become a family. During the time of waiting, God was preparing our hearts for what He had in store for us. God knows exactly what we need and exactly when we need it, but sometimes, it requires a little bit of patience while waiting.

SET

"The Lord visited Sarah as he had said, and the Lord did to Sarah as he had promised. And Sarah conceived and bore Abraham a son in his old age at the time of which God had spoken to him. Abraham called the name of his son who was born to him, whom Sarah bore him, Isaac."

Genesis 21:1-3

"But if we hope for what we do not see, we wait for it with patience. Likewise, the Spirit helps us in our weakness. For we do not know what to pray for as we ought, but the Spirit himself intercedes for us with groanings too deep for words."

Romans 8:25-26

GROW

Sarah and Abraham waited for a son for seventy-five years. That is a long time! Many people do not even live this long! Sarah desperately wanted a son and had to wait until she was ninety years old for God to give her Isaac. God is faithful to keep His promises and will reward those who patiently wait. Sarah's patience was indeed rewarded, and now her story is an example for all believers. This week, read the story of Sarah and Abraham in Genesis 21. Journal below how you think Sarah must have felt before and after finding out she was going to give birth to her son, Isaac. I pray Abraham and Sarah's story will inspire you to wait on the Lord with patience.

READY

One of my favorite pastors, Mike Haman, once said, "You do not have to cross the sea to see the cross." We are often led to believe that "true" missionaries are those who travel to far-off places in the world. The very idea of missions is often associated with traveling – "going on a missions trip." For sure, many missionaries answer God's call to leave home and serve His people throughout the world. All over the world, there are immeasurable needs waiting to be met by the hands and feet of Christ.

Thankfully, there are also opportunities right at our fingertips to show the love of Christ. Missionaries who choose to travel to other countries to spread God's word are much needed, but we also need people who are willing to work right where they are. Before you embark on a big trip to serve others, try serving in your community first. A dear family friend of mine was diagnosed with a rare form of cancer in her shoulder and had to undergo a very traumatic, life-changing surgery. The doctors had to remove her scapula to ensure that the cancer was gone. She lost mobility and strength in her right arm. She also went through six very tough rounds of chemotherapy. To encourage her throughout chemotherapy, my mom, my brothers, and I went to chalk her driveway. We drew hearts, flowers, and rainbows until the entire box of chalk was empty. My family and I are not artists, but this was a simple, enjoyable way to brighten her day. We were able to completely fill her driveway in no time! In addition, we were able to serve her in other simple ways, like preparing meals, spending time with her

kids, and helping with household chores. It was a great opportunity to show Christ's love locally.

Recognizing opportunities to love others can be a challenge. We must see things the way Jesus would and share His mindset. To discover the Lord's mindset, dig into Scripture. Study how Jesus lived His life. No matter what Jesus did, it was evident He always put other people before Himself. It did not matter if they were of a different race or culture, younger, older, or weaker than He. Because of Jesus's humble service, "God elevated Him to the highest place of honor and gave Him the name above all other names" (Philippians 2:9). I challenge you to live differently. Focus on the people around you. God has placed you exactly where you are for a reason. You were created to make a difference. He will use you in mighty ways to expand His kingdom right where you are! Do not worry about having to cross the sea to see the cross. God is needed everywhere, and He has enabled you to bless others right where you are.

SET

"And he answered, 'You shall love the Lord your God with all your heart and with all your soul and with all your strength and with all your mind, and your neighbor as yourself.'"

Luke 10:27

GROW

If you are curious who your neighbor is, I encourage you to read the rest of Jesus's parable on the Good Samaritan found in Luke 10:25-37. Jesus may be placing missionary opportunities in your path today. You do not have to look far. Ask God to give you the heart to recognize opportunities to show Christ's love, and write at least three opportunities you can embrace this week in the space provided below. He will bless you for blessing others.

READY

Has anyone ever told you, "You're crazy!"?

Let me tell you about some craziness involving our family vacation. A few days after Thanksgiving, we traveled to the beach. Since Christmas was right around the corner, my mom brought each of us matching Christmas pajamas and Santa hats to wear while we were on vacation. My mom suggested that we walk out onto the beach with our Christmas pajamas and hats to take a silly Christmas picture. Each family member had a different reaction. My sister, my youngest brother, and my dad all had strong opinions about this idea. They all agreed that we would look absolutely ridiculous and that taking a picture on the beach with our Christmas jammies would be embarrassing. My mom, my oldest brother, and I all agreed that taking a silly family picture would be fun and that we would create such an awesome memory. Since the family was equally split on the issue, we ultimately decided to take the picture to make Mom happy (and so she would stop mentioning the idea to us all the time ☺). Thankfully, as we walked down to the beach, not many people stopped and stared at us, but the three people in my family who voted "no" were still extremely embarrassed. We got a staff member at the resort to take the photo, and then as soon as we were done, my youngest brother, my sister, and my dad literally ran back to the room! On her way to our room, my sister received a few compliments from some other guests who said that taking a family picture in Christmas pajamas was such a great idea.

Often, we are afraid to put ourselves out there. Half of my family was worried about other people's opinions as we took a silly picture on the beach. However, the other half of my family was focused on enjoying the moment. Sometimes, the opinions of others stand in the way of our ability to recognize the opportunities God has placed in our lives. As Paul commands in Colossians, we must set our minds on things above and focus on what God thinks of us. To Him, we are precious, valued, and loved. Unlike God's unchanging love, other people's opinions change all the time. Be crazy for Christ by putting yourself out there for His glory.

SET

"Set your minds on things that are above, not on things that are on earth."

Colossians 3:12

"Do not be conformed to this world, but be transformed by the renewal of your mind, that by testing you may discern what is the will of God, what is good and acceptable and perfect."

Romans 12:2

GROW

I challenge you this week to memorize Colossians 3:12 and highlight it in your Bible. Write down ways you can block out voices that are hindering you from embracing the opportunities God has placed in your life. For me, those voices are sometimes others' opinions. It is easy to let what other people think prohibit us from stepping into what God has planned for us, but I challenge you to allow God's voice to surpass them all. Listen to Him and obey His calling for you this week.

READY

At the end of my 8th grade school year, several moms hosted a dance at a local venue to celebrate our graduation. I am not a fan of school dances...at all! But of course, all my friends convinced me to go, I had a date, and my mom was one of the chaperones. Basically, I felt like I had no choice. As soon as I got there, I knew in my spirit something was not right, but I just said to myself, "Hannah Beth, you've just got to do this!" As the night progressed from dinner to the dance, the DJ began playing music. As I listened to the songs, I could not believe what I was hearing. Even my friend's mom who was also chaperoning was concerned about the music. She whispered in my ear, "Are you hearing these words, too?!" The music was very inappropriate, and everyone there was dancing and singing along, not paying attention to the actual song lyrics. I went up to my mom within the first five minutes (thank goodness she was chaperoning, which I now can see was God's provision), and told her that we needed to go. I could not listen to that music because I felt God was telling me to guard my heart, and I knew that the song lyrics were not in agreement with God's word. My mom and I "went to the bathroom" as an excuse and then left. I did not regret leaving...in fact, I felt relief as we pulled away.

We are responsible for guarding our hearts. Our parents may advise us not to be in certain places or do certain things; however, ultimately, it is our choice. We can gather opinions and thoughts from others, but ultimately, we must develop the

skill to discern right from wrong. We do this by connecting with Jesus through prayer and meditating on His Word. When we are in communion with God and know His truths and promises, we are prepared to make decisions that honor and glorify God. As Christians, our goal is to reflect Christ by doing the right thing. Guarding your heart can be difficult, especially with all the distractions and temptations. If you feel as if you are in a questionable situation, ask yourself "Does this honor God?" If the answer is no, then remove yourself from the situation and seek His wisdom. As you draw closer

to Him, you will find yourself further from such situations.
Never stop talking to God! Guarding your heart is crucial because
everything we do flows from the heart, and we want our actions
to reflect Christ.

SET

"Keep your heart with all vigilance,
for from it flow the springs of life."

Proverbs 4:23

"And the peace of God, which surpasses all
understanding, will guard your hearts and
your minds in Christ Jesus."

Philippians 4:7

GROW

If we want our actions and words to reflect Christ, then we need to protect our hearts from people or things that contradict God and His Word. Proverbs 4:23 speaks of vigilance, which is defined as "the action or state of keeping careful watch for possible dangers or difficulties." I challenge you to memorize this verse. Write it below three times in your favorite color. It is only 13 words, and it will remind you that the heart is very precious. We must guard it because our words, thoughts, and actions flow from what we value in our hearts.

The definition of a "miracle" from Merriam-Webster is: "1: an extraordinary event manifesting divine intervention in human affairs, the healing miracles described in the Gospels. 2: an extremely outstanding or unusual event, thing, or accomplishment." I find it interesting that the worldly definition of miracles began with the Gospels. God invented miracles and designed them to immediately draw humans into His awesome presence. God's miracles can be found both in the Old Testament as God interacted with His chosen people and in the Gospels during Jesus's life on earth.

The Bible is full of "extraordinary events." For instance, consider the birth of Abraham and Sarah's son, Isaac. Sarah was 90 and Abraham was 100 when their son was born. Sarah laughed at the possibility of God giving her a child at her age, yet God remained faithful and gave them a son despite their doubt. Before Isaac was brought into this world, God promised Abraham and Sarah that they would have as many descendants as there are stars in the sky. God will always fulfill His promises in His timing.

My life has been personally touched by a "divine intervention in human affairs," specifically the circumstances surrounding my birth. My original due date was June 10th; however, I was born April 3rd. I came into this world weighing a tiny two pounds and six ounces! I was considered premature, and because of the seriousness of the situation, both my mom and I were considered high-risk. My mom's preeclampsia, which is

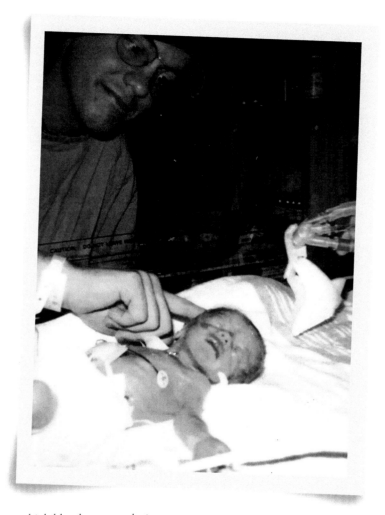

high blood pressure during pregnancy,
forced her to have an emergency C- section. The only way her health
would improve was to deliver me, but I was nowhere near ready
to enter this world because I was not fully developed. Immediately

after my delivery, I had to be airlifted to another local hospital with a higher level neo-natal intensive care unit. I stayed there for five weeks, and I finally came home weighing four pounds and six ounces! Thankfully, my mom and I both survived and have remained healthy since. Many premature babies are at risk for hearing and vision problems, impaired learning, and other chronic health issues, but I am so blessed to say that I have not experienced any of these problems. This is a miracle for which I continue to praise God each day of my life.

God has been performing miracles since creation began. Some of these are large and public and others are small and intimate. Regardless, all miracles reveal what is most important: God's love. Each miracle is God thoughtfully intervening on behalf of His people.

SET

"He is your praise. He is your God, who has done for you these great and terrifying things that your eyes have seen."

Deuteronomy 10:21

GROW

Have you experienced any miracles? They may be in your life, in others' lives, or in God's word. Make a list below of miracles you have witnessed and thank God for each one. Recognizing miracles helps us grow our faith and allows us to understand more about Him. If you are ever doubting the reality of miracles, just remember, YOU – your life, your being, your existence – are a miracle, too!

READY

I am about to tell you one of the most embarrassing things that has ever happened to me in my entire life. This happened almost twenty-four hours before I wrote this devotion. I was returning home from running camp, and I had just said goodbye to my teammates. As I looked to make sure no one was behind me, I saw several of my teammates give me a thumbs-up that I was clear to back up. I pulled out of the parking spot and began to slowly move forward. I did not see anything in front of me as I drove forward, but suddenly, I heard loud scratching and thumping noises and thought to myself, "Oh, great... I definitely just hit something." As I put my car in park and stepped out, I noticed very quickly that everyone was looking at me wide-eyed and shocked. I was terrified to see three bags, a pillow, a bookbag, a can of cream soda, and other various items scattered under my car. I had run over a teammate's luggage from the trip! Everyone was staring at me, and I just wanted to cry. Thankfully, nothing valuable was damaged. My teammate was very forgiving and did not seem worried about his flattened items. After realizing everything was okay, everyone burst out laughing!

In life, sometimes we can lose sight of what is in front of us because we are distracted. If we do not lift our eyes up and acknowledge these things, we will eventually run over them. They will trip us up, doing damage to ourselves and others. Do not wait until you have hit an issue to deal with it. Instead, keep your eyes focused ahead on what God has called you to

so that you can avoid the potholes in life. The good thing is, no matter where you are driving, who is with you, or what is in front of you, God is the one riding in the passenger seat WITH YOU! He has the map and knows the best path forward. If you listen to Him and let him navigate, your journey will be blessed. You will avoid needless potholes, overcome challenging obstacles, and arrive at a glorious destination!

"My help comes from the LORD,
who made heaven and earth."

Psalms 121:2

"It is the Lord who goes before you. He will be with you; he will not leave you or forsake you. Do not fear or be dismayed."

Deuteronomy 31:8

"Whether you turn to the right or to the left, your ears will hear a voice behind you saying, 'This is the way; walk in it.'"

Isaiah 30:21

GROW

In the space below, identify something in your life that might be blocking your path. Just like your teachers probably tell you not to procrastinate with your schoolwork, God does not want you to procrastinate about taking action with what He has in store for you. Set up a plan to face this obstacle and successfully deal with this challenge. Ask for His help in recognizing and addressing the obstacles in your life.

READY

What types of books do you love to read: adventure, biography, history, mystery, war, action, romance? There is one book that contains all these genres and more. It is the best seller of all time – the Bible! For some, the Bible is a very boring, outdated book full of "thee" and "thou," long-winded family trees, and rules upon rules. However, as I have spent more time with God's word, I have come to appreciate that the Bible is full of amazing stories. It has acts of betrayal, tales of redemption, and miracles galore. There are spies, adulterers, murderers, and more. The Bible even has a talking donkey!

While many of the stories in the Bible are entertaining, the true purpose of these stories is to convey God's unending love for us. The Bible reveals God's character and shows the extent to which He will go to pursue us. It tells the story of redemption which is symbolized by the cross. I guess you could call the stories of redemption "cross-words!" According to Hebrews 4:12, the Bible is "living and active." Therefore, even though it was written by multiple authors thousands of years ago, God's word is still relevant for us today. God is not limited by time and neither is His word. If you seek true wisdom and understanding in your life, I recommend that you spend time with the Bible. If you need encouragement or confidence, go to the word. God tells His people to dwell on the word day and night (Psalm 1:2). My pastor would call this

"marinating in the word." When we consistently
focus on God's word, we begin to understand the ways in which we
are called to speak, act, and think.

"For the word of God is living and active, sharper than any two-edged sword, piercing to the division of soul and of spirit, of joints and of marrow, and discerning the thoughts and intentions of the heart."

Hebrews 4:12

"The grass withers, the flower fades, but the word of our God will stand forever."

Isaiah 40:8

"Heaven and earth will pass away, but my words will not pass away."

Matthew 24:35

GROW

This week I wanted to share with you a special picture of my great-grandfather's Bible *(pictured on page 55)*. It has been in our family for seven generations and is believed to be from the mid-1800's! After my great-grandfather died, his Bible was passed down to my dad. It is a family heirloom that we cherish dearly. While the cover and pages show obvious wear, the words within are untouched by age. This week I encourage you to spend extra time with God's word. Write below the names of five of your favorite stories from the Bible and commit to read one each day this week.

READY

One of the only times I remember being nervous in elementary school was during P.E. The teacher would pick two team captains, and they would choose members to join their teams. I was always afraid of being picked last. Captains always pick the best first – whether that is their best friend or the best player. Those picked last are really not chosen – they are simply the last option available. Thankfully with God, we were His first choice!

Merriam-Webster defines "chosen" as "having been selected as the best or most appropriate." Although we all fall short of the glory of God, He chooses us because He sees us for who He has created us to be—His children. He loves YOU more than you can even fathom. He desires to manifest Himself within YOUR heart. None of us are worthy of being chosen by God, but His wonderful, never-ending grace extends to all people. There is nothing you can do to change God's grace and love for you. Also, you will never be "unchosen" by God. Before you were born, God chose you, and He will never stop choosing you because that is just who He is. No sin is big enough for God to let you go. In fact, it is in our weakness that we can see His strength! Nothing will ever separate YOU from the love of Christ. You can run from Him, but you cannot hide, because He is already in your hiding place waiting for you with arms wide open. He will always love YOU, and you cannot do anything to change that. I want to encourage you to embrace the love God has for you.

The moment you realize how much He truly loves you, you will be astonished!

I remember one day I was driving home from school after practice and a Christian song called "Joy," by Tori Harper started playing. I began to cry. I never cry! During this moment, I was reminded I am not worthy of Christ's love, yet He gives it to me freely. I was reminded that I am chosen by God, not because of anything I have done, but because of all that He has done. His blood was shed for me, you, and every other person on this earth so that our sins could be forgiven. Now we have the opportunity to experience eternal life with

Him in heaven. After the song ended, I thanked God for who He is, His love for me, and His decision to choose me. I encourage you to do the same.

SET

"You did not choose me, but I chose you and appointed you that you should go and bear fruit and that your fruit should abide, so that whatever you ask the Father in my name, he may give it to you." John 15:16

"Just as He chose us in Him before the foundation of the world, that we would be holy and blameless before Him In love."

Ephesians 1:4

"But you are a chosen race, A royal priesthood, a holy nation, a people for God's own possession, so that you may proclaim the excellencies of Him who has called you out of darkness into His marvelous light."

1 Peter 2:9

"No, in all these things we are more than conquerors through him who loved us. For I am sure that neither death nor life, nor angels nor rulers, nor things present nor things to come, nor powers, nor height nor depth, nor anything else in all creation, will be able to separate us from the love of God in Christ Jesus our Lord."

Romans 8:37-39

GROW

We are chosen by God and nothing can ever separate us from His amazing love. I challenge you to truly believe that God chose you. I encourage you to live each day like a chosen child of the King because that is who you are! Listen to "Joy" by Tori Harper. Thank God for choosing and loving you despite your sins, flaws, weaknesses, and unworthiness. Can you complete these lyrics from the song?

Your joy is greater than ....

....

Your love will conquer ....

....

....

READY

Because I have lived in seven states, God has given me opportunities to meet lots of people from all over the world. I am very grateful I have developed many different friendships. Between our move from Georgia to North Carolina, I prayed to God asking for at least one good friend. He exceeded my expectations by blessing me with many amazing friends in North Carolina. Good friends are gifts from God and the rarest of treasures! He designed us for community with others and calls us to love one another. I have learned that to have a good friend, you must be a good friend. Being a good friend involves several steps. Our church's benediction explains these steps very well: *"Upward, Inward, Outward."*

"UPWARD" stands for loving God completely. Matthew 22:37 says, "Love the Lord your God with all your heart, soul, mind, and strength." To know how to love others, we must look to Christ. By dying on the cross for all sinners, He demonstrated the ultimate act of love. When we learn to love God completely, He shows us how to love others. *"INWARD"* refers to loving yourself correctly. Loving yourself correctly is realizing and accepting who you are in Christ. In Matthew 22:39, God commands us to "love [our] neighbor[s] as [ourselves]." If we cannot love ourselves the correct way, we are unable to love others properly, either. When you see yourself as Christ does, you can then begin to love others as Christ loves you. *"OUTWARD"* calls us to love others around us compassionately.

Obviously, being a good friend requires
that you show your love and care for the other person. We are called
to care about the well-being of others by loving them well.

These three steps, *Upward, Inward,* and *Outward*, help us become
a better friend and a stronger follower of Christ. Jesus perfected
this process. Scripture tells us He clearly worshipped the Father, He
recognized His value as the Son, and He showed compassion to all in
need. We will never have a better friend than Jesus. He knows more
about us than we know about ourselves – even the number of hairs on

our head (Luke 12:7). Follow His example and strive to love others the way Christ loves us. Friends are gifts from God, so let's treat them this way.

SET

"Therefore be imitators of God, as beloved children. And walk in love, as Christ loved us and gave himself up for us, a fragrant offering and sacrifice to God."
Ephesians 5:1-2

"Why, even the hairs of your head are all numbered."
Luke 12:7

GROW

This week, I challenge you to pray about ways you can become a better friend. In fact, asking other people this question is a great idea. When you can determine your strengths and weaknesses from others' perspectives, you will get a better idea of how to improve. Write what you believe to be your strengths and weaknesses in friendship below. Then ask a friend to list your strengths and weaknesses and compare the lists.

READY

One of my favorite sayings is, "It's the little things in life." This has certainly proved true in my life. For instance, my sophomore year, I was scratched from the 4x800 relay team at the track conference championship because of an injury. Fifteen minutes before the race began, I was limping during warmups; therefore, my coach quickly had to find an alternate runner to take my spot. Thankfully, a good friend of mine was willing to run in my place. I wanted to run badly - not just for myself, but for my team and ultimately for God. I was so upset that I began to tear up, and if you know me well enough, you know that I rarely cry. For me, the realization that I would not be running in the conference or the upcoming state meet left me discouraged; however, the feelings of disappointment began to vanish as two of my teammates came up to me. They gave me a hug and said, "HB, I know injuries are hard, but once you recover, you are going to come back stronger than ever." Although this does not seem like much, it encouraged my heart and challenged me to change my mindset during my rehab. Instead of focusing on what I wished to be doing, which was running, I decided to focus on encouraging my teammates as they ran. This injury also changed my perspective. I realized that my injury was a small, temporary setback in the big scheme of life. God has every situation in his hands, including this one.

What did I learn from my teammates? We should always remember that our words and actions, even if they are small,

can make a big difference in someone else's life. I like to put it this way: "Sometimes, it takes something small at the start to grow something big in the finish." In fact, God can take anything small and transform it into something big. For example, inviting a friend to youth group is a simple act, but it could lead to an encounter with Jesus that could change lives. The next time you see the opportunity to encourage someone in a simple way, don't question yourself or hesitate. Listen to the Holy Spirit because our all-powerful God can use you and your words to help others in mighty ways.

"He put another parable before them, saying, 'The kingdom of heaven is like a grain of mustard seed that a man took and sowed in his field. It is the smallest of all seeds, but when it has grown it is larger than all the garden plants and becomes a tree, so that the birds of the air come and make nests in its branches.'"

Matthew 13:31-32)

"And we know that for those who love God all things work together for good, for those called according to His purpose."

Romans 8:28

GROW

Our words and actions are like seeds. Get busy planting and see what God grows! I challenge you this week to encourage a friend, family member, teacher, student, or even a stranger with a little act of kindness. It does not have to be huge; it is the "little things." It could be a friendly smile, an encouraging note or text, or paying for someone's meal behind you in the drive-thru line. We need to make sure our kind actions do not have to be seen by others. List three little acts of kindness that you can do for someone else, and check them off as you complete them. Whatever it may be, even if it seems small, trust that God will use it to make a big difference.

READY

My brother, Noah, is very interested in the weather. If my family cannot find Noah, it is safe to assume he is somewhere watching the Weather Channel or checking the forecast. Forecasting the weather is like predicting the future. Wouldn't we all like the ability to forecast the future? We would know what the day holds before we opened our eyes each morning. We could find comfort and security in knowing what the day ahead brings. I would feel much more relaxed if a teacher told me about a test two weeks before the test date than if a teacher started class by giving a pop quiz. We like to know the future ahead of time, so that we can prepare ourselves for the events to come. Thankfully, with the Weather Channel as a quick and easy resource, we know how to dress and can prepare accordingly. Events such as sports games, meetings, and social gatherings, are placed on the calendar ahead of time to ensure that we remember them. Despite all this planning and forecasting, there are times when we are simply unable to properly prepare. What if you got sick the day of a big dance performance? Maybe your friend cancelled your plans at the last minute? Unexpected things in life happen all the time, causing our plans to change. Likewise, we cannot always count on the Weather Channel forecast because it is just a prediction. We must remember that God alone determines all outcomes.

One of the biggest and most impactful surprises during my lifetime has been COVID-19. Like many others, I had great

plans for 2020 – running track, prom, vacation,
attending church in person, and much more. COVID-19 flipped
all those plans upside down. Instead, 2020 has been about wearing
masks, quarantining, washing our hands, and staying six feet apart.
For some, it has been much tougher and more serious, as they have
battled the symptoms of COVID-19 or grieved the loss of loved
ones who were overcome by the virus. It is not the year we expected.
Often, we think one thing, and life serves us the complete opposite.
While we might not know what is coming, be encouraged that God

does. God is in control, and He is working everything out for the good of those who love Him (Romans 8:28). Trust in the Lord always, no matter what the forecast, and grow through what you go through.

"Even before a word is on my tongue, behold, O Lord, you know it altogether."

Psalm 139:4

"He determines the number of the stars; he gives to all of them their names."

Psalm 147:4

"Many are the afflictions of the righteous, but the Lord delivers him out of them all."

Psalm 34:19

GROW

My favorite time to be outside is when the sky is blue, the sun is shining, and the temperature is around 70 degrees. This is my ideal weather for each day; however, where I live, the weather can vary greatly throughout the seasons. The different types of weather are like the seasons of our lives. We must learn to embrace all kinds of weather as we go through each season. For fun, draw your favorite weather condition in the space provided below. Review the three verses for this week and write your favorite above your weather report. As you draw, ask the Lord to help you trust in His plan for your life, not your own.

READY

I hope you noticed that "for" is emphasized in this title. Usually, "for" is not a word of emphasis, but in this case, it is very important. The Bible says that God is FOR you. God fights FOR His people all the time. As a 2 pounds, 6 ounces premature baby, I was completely helpless. The doctors thought I would survive but predicted I would probably endure many trials along the way due to my prematurity. The only explanation for the fact that I am alive and healthy is that God was fighting FOR me. If He fights FOR me, He fights FOR you, too. He is on your side, not only fighting WITH you, but fighting FOR you.

It is important not to look to your circumstances as a reflection of whether God is "for" you. It is easy to mistake difficult circumstances for the loss of God's favor in your life. Some are even tempted to think that their tough circumstances might even be a sign that God is against them. Find encouragement in the fact that your circumstances do not reflect God's love. God's character and faithfulness are never changing, no matter the circumstances. Every day we are faced with battles. Some may be bigger than others, but God can help us defeat the enemy at any time, under any circumstances. We do not deserve to have Him on our side, yet He is there, fighting FOR us. Trust God in spite of your circumstances. Do not fix your eyes on your situation; instead, fix them on the cross. He died to fight FOR you.

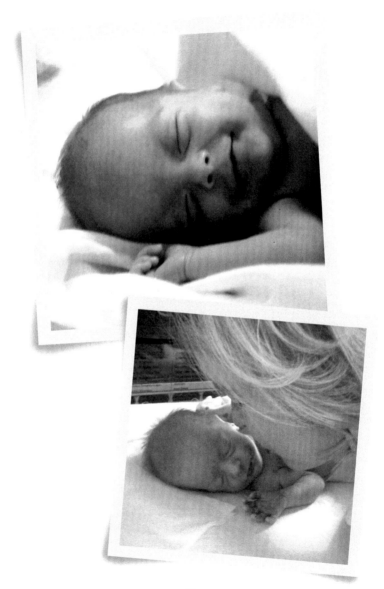

"What then shall we say to these things?
If God is for us, who can be against us?"

Romans 8:31

"Fear not, for I am with you; be not dismayed,
for I am your God; I will strengthen you, I
will help you, I will uphold you with my
righteous right hand."

Isaiah 41:10

"I can do all things through Him
who strengthens me."

Philippians 4:13

GROW

People and circumstances may be against us, but God will fight FOR us, strengthen us, and hold us up with His righteous hand. In order to hold your hand, God must be standing right beside you! He is FOR you and WITH you! The song, "Our God" by Chris Tomlin will remind you that there is no one else who fights FOR you like God does! Listen to this song at least once a day this week and let the beautiful lyrics fill your heart with the truth that God is always FOR you. Also, I challenge you to write a prayer asking God to fight FOR you in all your battles. Here is an example:

Dear Lord,
I want to ask You to fight FOR me in all my battles, whether they are big or small. I trust You with my life and circumstances, and I ask that You use them to honor You. I want to thank You for being on my side, even though I am undeserving of Your love and grace. I love You, Lord, and thank You for being FOR me and not against me. In Your name I pray, Amen!

READY

Have you ever looked up the definition of love? We use the word "love" frequently; therefore, it is important that we understand its true meaning. According to the Merriam-Webster definition, love is "an intense feeling of deep affection for someone or something." I was intrigued because the word "deep" was used in the definition. Deep is a word I have been focusing on for the year. Loving others and God more deeply has been one of my goals.

My pastor, Dr. Derwin Gray, has repeatedly said that he will never stop talking about love in his sermons because God is love (1 John 4:7). The world tries to twist and cheapen love, offering many counterfeits. However, any love that is not of God or from God is not real love. Christianity begins with love, and from love flows all other Christ-like qualities. Love serves as the foundation of our lives as Christians. It is also significant because we were designed for love! We are created by God to love and to be loved.

Across the world, the universal symbol for love is a heart. I wish the "cross" were our symbol for love because it is the greatest act of love ever! When we think of love, the cross should come to our mind first. The human heart is sinful, but God purifies our hearts through His love. God sent His one and only Son who is pure and blameless to die on the cross for us all *while we were still sinners* (Romans 5:8). I emphasized the last part of the previous sentence because I want you to realize that Jesus did not die for people who were worthy. We have

never deserved any of God's love and we never will. God *gave* us salvation which means that we do not have to earn it. Now that is what I call LOVE! Despite your sins or your past, He loves you right where you are, and He has never loved you any more or any less.

Love is not just a feeling or an emotion. Feelings and emotions are fleeting and deceptive and often lead us astray. Love is ultimately a choice and a commitment. You cannot always have wonderful "feelings" for a person, but you can always choose to have love. In fact, Jesus did not want to die on the cross. He asked his Father, God "if you are willing, take this cup from me; yet not my will but yours" (Luke 22:42). I am so grateful that Jesus did not rely on His feelings but instead on a choice to obey!

SET

"We love because He first loved us."

1 John 4:19

"But God shows his love for us in that while we were still sinners, Christ died for us."

Romans 5:8

"For by grace you have been saved through faith. And this is not your own doing; it is the gift of God."

Ephesians 2:8

GROW

The Bible contains the word *love* over 500 times. I challenge you to remember this week that you are loved by Christ. Look up some of the following verses about love (John 3:16, John 14:21, John 15:9, 1 John 4:9-10, 1 John 4:12, 1 John 4:16, Psalm 36:7, Galatians 2:20 , Romans 5:5, Romans 5:8, Romans 8:38-39). Highlight in your Bible each time you see the word *love*. Write your favorite verse below. Use this truth to encourage yourself to love others like God has loved you. Stand firm in the love of Christ and remember that Love = God!

READY

One of the most exciting things about turning sixteen is the ability to get a driver's license. From that point forward, your license becomes your most frequent form of photo identification. However, your driver's license only has a few characteristics that identify you – hair color, height, age, organ donor status; but, this is not your identity. Our full identity includes the qualities, beliefs, and personality traits that describe us. The most important of all these attributes is our identity in Christ. When we say that our identity lies in Christ, we are saying Christ is in us and defines us. When we give our lives to Jesus, He transforms us into a new creation. He renews our hearts and washes us clean of all sin. When we become Christ's children through baptism and accept Him as our Savior, what is true about Christ becomes true of us! When we are claimed by Christ, God sees us in the same way He sees Jesus. Isn't that amazing?! To say our identity is in Christ means that we are one with Christ. We share the same qualities and characteristics as Jesus. The Bible tells us Christ is holy, loved, unique, precious, and valued. These are true of us as well! As we turn our lives over to Him, His qualities begin to manifest themselves in us and affect the way we live. Jesus changes people! It is an honor that God views us in the same way He sees Jesus. He looks past our sins and sees Jesus. He values us not because of what we have accomplished, but because of who we are: children of God.

Many people find their identity in other places such as school, sports, extracurriculars, family, friends, social media, and

achievements. For example, I believe some, including myself, are tempted to place their identity in how well they perform academically or athletically. It is easy to believe that our identity lies in these areas because this is how we are often measured and rewarded by the world.

With running, I often think to myself, "If I can just run faster," or "If I could just beat those girls, that would be enough." However, the only thing that will truly be enough is Jesus Christ and His love. Instead of placing our identity elsewhere, always remember your identity lies in Christ, and the greatest reward you will ever receive is your crown in heaven. We share identity with Jesus! We are one with the God who created all of earth, formed humans from dust, sent His Son to die on the cross, loves us unconditionally, forgives us of our sins, and continually washes waves of mercy on us each day. This is the identity of OUR amazing God.

SET

"But to all who did receive him, to those who believed in his name, he gave the right to become children of God."

John 1:12

GROW

Because we have identity in Christ, we should do two things. First, we should thank the Lord that He accepts us where we are as sinners. Second, we should let Christ saturate our lives so that His identity covers us. When we accept Him into our hearts, we become children of God and share His identity. Remind yourself every day this week that you share an identity with our amazing Lord. List at least three qualities you share with Christ. Now list one quality that you strive to share with Christ. Believe the truth the Bible says about Jesus and remember that is true of you, too!

READY

Excellence is simple to define yet hard to achieve. My family's definition of excellence is *doing* the best with what God has given you. However, we often mistake "excellence" for *being* perfect in everything we do. This is a recipe for disappointment. My freshman, sophomore, and junior years of high school were academically challenging. I chose to take harder classes because I wanted to do well like the top students in my grade, so I spent hours upon hours sitting at my kitchen counter studying and completing homework. I was able to achieve good grades in my classes; however, the amount of time I spent trying to match the academic achievements of my classmates was unnecessary and excessive. Some people thrive in an academically rigorous environment, but God reminded me I had to balance my workload.

Heading into my senior year, I decided to take classes that would be challenging, but not overbearing. I was tired of the academic stress and intense competition for top grades. The academic pressure during my first three years caused me to lose sight of my other gifts from God. I realized that God gave me a heart to serve and love others. I decided during my senior year to devote more time to my God-given passions to honor Him. The academic workload during my senior year has still been challenging, but it is much less time consuming than my previous years. The best part is that I have been able to be involved in more activities that align with my passions. I have served as a chaplain, I have joined a service outreach class called Contain-It, and I have been able to pursue my love for

others by spending more time with friends and family.

Rather than sitting for hours at my kitchen counter, I have had an enjoyable senior year not simply because I decided to take a few easier classes, but because I have accepted the Lord's view of excellence. I have realized not everyone can pursue academic achievement to its highest level. God calls us to do our best with what He has given to us, not to desire what He did not give us. When we pursue excellence by using the gifts He has given us, we are showing honor to the Lord.

"Whatever you do, work at it with all your heart, as working for the Lord, not for men."

Colossians 3:23

"Therefore, be imitators of God, as beloved children."

Ephesians 5:1

"So, whether you eat or drink, or whatever you do, do all to the glory of God."

1 Corinthians 10:31

GROW

I encourage you to give your best effort in all you do and remember that God is the Provider for your strength and abilities. God will bless you when He sees your hard work and obedience. God created the entire world and has sustained it. His excellence surpasses all. Journal below a list of your special gifts. How can you use these gifts to glorify God?

READY

If you look up the statistics on how many people have compared themselves to others, you will find results of 100%. I will admit that I have compared myself to friends who are smarter, teammates who are faster and stronger, and Christians who are more devoted to their faith. All people have compared themselves to someone else, whether they realize it or not. Our world is full of comparisons, which makes them hard to avoid. Someone who is constantly comparing often feels depressed. It is important not to compare ourselves to others because God has given each of us certain abilities for a purpose. He did not randomly assign your gifts; He carefully chose your unique talents and characteristics. We are created as one body; however, we are given unique gifts to further His Kingdom.

How should we avoid comparison? First, we need to be self-aware. We should be confident in our God-given strengths and aware of our weaknesses. Be grateful for the strengths God has given you and use them to bless others and serve the Lord. Second, instead of comparing ourselves to other people, we should compliment others. Encouraging others through compliments is simple, and it has the power to bring tremendous joy! Words have the potential to build people up or tear people down, so choose your words wisely. Third, be willing to ask for help. Most people fear asking for help because they are afraid of looking "weak." Asking for help is a sign of strength because it shows you realize your weaknesses and desire to improve.

I have never excelled in math and have always needed help.
However, my dad is practically a math genius, so I often use him as
my math tutor. Because I go to my dad seeking improvement and better
understanding, I typically receive the help I need to do my best. For
example, I took Pre-Calculus my junior year of high school. At our
end of the year awards ceremony, I was absolutely shocked to hear
my name called when they announced the highest average for college
prep Pre-Calculus. My parents almost fainted they were so surprised.

By studying and working hard, I was able to thrive in something that does not come naturally to me. Just like I asked my dad to help me with math, asking God to help you is the most important step.

SET

"As each has received a gift, use it to serve one another, as good stewards of God's varied grace."

1 Peter 4:10

"I praise you, for I am fearfully and wonderfully made. Wonderful are your works; my soul knows it very well."

Psalm 139:14

The next time you find yourself comparing yourself to others, hold yourself accountable by:

1. Being self-aware (God has created you fearfully and wonderfully in your mother's womb)

2. Complimenting others

3. Asking the Lord to provide the help you need to improve

I challenge you to apply these three steps to avoid comparison in all aspects of your life. If you work on doing these three things instead of comparing, you will experience God's peace that surpasses all understanding (Philippians 4:7). Write down the names of at least three people to whom you have compared yourself and commit to complimenting them. When you find yourself comparing, remember God has given you amazing gifts, too, and He wants you to use them to further His Kingdom.

READY

For many people, the Christian faith is seen as a set of rules and good works that we must adhere to. Some may say you need to read the Bible, pray, and go to church every Sunday to find favor with God. Others will point to the Ten Commandments as the measuring stick for faith.

I have been prone to thinking that the greater amount of good things I "do" will help me become a better Christian. Thankfully, the Lord has recently awakened my heart to recognize this untruth. He humbled my spirit and allowed me to see that the good things I "do" are not what truly matters. Our faith in Jesus is the only thing that saves us. God has called us to a faith that is bigger than rules and actions. He has called us to a personal relationship. He created us in His image and sees us covered by the resurrection of His own Son, Jesus. Reading God's word, praying, and going to church are all wonderful ways to grow in your relationship with Christ, and it is important to do each of these things. However, these actions do not make God love you any more or less. Likewise, the Ten Commandments in Exodus 20 are not requirements to get into heaven. God designed these for our personal well-being. Obeying Christ's commands and doing good deeds overflow out of our faith; but they are NOT the methods of achieving salvation. As Jesus says, "I am the way, the truth, and the life, and the only way to the Father is through me" (John 14:6). In other words, it does not matter how many service hours you log, how many people you encourage each day, or how many times you attend church each month. All that matters is that

you profess your faith in
Jesus's life, death, and resurrection.

Do rules and works not matter? Of course they do! In James 2:14-26,
we see that faith and good deeds work together. When we know and
love God, we want to obey God's law and honor him. James 2:26
reminds us that "faith apart from works is dead." As Christians, we
should strive to glorify God in all our actions, but we do not gain God's
approval or earn His love through our performance. Be encouraged
that you cannot work your way into heaven...admittance is only by
the free gift of salvation that comes through Christ.

"Jesus said to him, "I am the way, and the truth, and the life. No one comes to the Father except through me."

John 14:6

"What good is it, my brothers, if someone says he has faith but does not have works? Can that faith save him? If a brother or sister is poorly clothed and lacking in daily food, and one of you says to them, "Go in peace, be warmed and filled," without giving them the things needed for the body, what good is that? So also faith by itself, if it does not have works, is dead. But someone will say, "You have faith and I have works." Show me your faith apart from your works, and I will show you my faith by my works. You believe that God is one; you do well. Even the demons believe—and shudder! Do you want to be shown, you foolish person, that faith apart from works is useless? Was not Abraham our father justified by works when he offered up his son Isaac on the altar? You see that faith was active along with his works, and faith was completed by his works; and the Scripture was fulfilled that says, "Abraham believed God, and it was counted to him as righteousness"—and he was called a friend of God. You see that a person is justified by works and not by faith alone. And in the same way was not also Rahab the prostitute justified by works when she received the messengers and sent them out by another way? For as the body apart from the spirit is dead, so also faith apart from works is dead."

James 2:14-26

GROW

James is one of my favorite books of the Bible. It contains five chapters full of wisdom. Read a chapter of James every day this week and highlight the verses that speak to your heart. If you have a favorite verse from James, please write it in the space provided.

READY

As I am currently writing this devotional, on June 22, 2019, I feel as if I have been knocked down – way down. Earlier this week, I had an MRI on my ankle, and the very next day I found out that I had a stress fracture. This is my second fracture in one year in the same spot as the previous injury, but on the other leg. My doctor told me to wear a boot and use crutches for two weeks (again). I already had to do this in the fall of 2018 due to a stress fracture at the beginning of my cross-country season. If I am being completely honest, I do not feel like I can do it again. The crutches and the boot wear me out physically, but this is especially difficult for me emotionally and even spiritually. As I was on the phone with my mom when she told me the news from the doctor, a million thoughts flooded my head. My first three questions included: "Why this whole thing again? With crutches and a boot, what activities can I still do to try to exercise? What good will come from this?"

I do not know why I am going through this whole thing again, BUT I do know that God has a plan. I have continued to pray that His will and not my own will be done in my life. During the MRI, I prayed almost the entire time that He uses me and my injury to glorify Himself and teach others. As I recovered, I discovered that there are exercises that I can still do! I taught myself to do one-legged planks and pushups, and I swam a lot! For the swimmers out there, I now have a deeper appreciation for you and your sport; it is a lot harder than it

looks! As for the third and final question: "What good could possibly come from this?" My coach told me, "Hannah Beth, many people view injuries as setbacks, but listen to me, I promise you they are not." Another phrase I have heard, that is similar to what my coach told me, is that "injuries aren't setbacks, they are set-ups." He told me that this injury is going to strengthen areas that are weak and ultimately, I will become stronger through this. That is hard to believe as I cannot imagine becoming a better runner without the ability to run.

Because of this injury, God reminded me that ultimately, He is the One who strengthens us. He is in control and holds us in the palm of

His hand. Although the feeling of getting knocked down is very hard, I encourage you to stay positive and focus on God. The good news is that once you are knocked down, the only direction to go is up. Jesus can take you further than you can imagine. While you may be disappointed, frustrated, or worried, trust that the God-ordained detours always lead to our destiny. You cannot see the end of the road, but He can, and we have to trust that He knows when it's best to stop, turn around, speed up, or slow down.

SET

"So do not fear, for I am with you; do not be dismayed, for I am your God. I will strengthen you and help you; I will uphold you with my right hand."   Isaiah 41:10

"Many are the plans in the mind of a man, but it is the purpose of the Lord that will stand."

Jeremiah 29:11

"We are afflicted in every way, but not crushed; perplexed, but not driven to despair; persecuted, but not forsaken; struck down, but not destroyed... So we do not lose heart. Though our outer self is wasting away, our inner self is being renewed day by day."

2 Corinthians 4:8-9, 16

GROW

If you feel as though you have been knocked down, do not give in to discouragement, because with God's strength, you can get back up again. He will always be there, and He has great, big plans waiting for you! Dwell on Isaiah 41:10 and Jeremiah 29:11. (*Dwell* has been one of my favorite words lately, and it means to keep your attention focused on something.) God desires us to dwell on His Scriptures so He can speak into our hearts. Which verse above speaks to you the most? Pick one to memorize this week and write it below. Ask Him to replace any lies you are believing about your setbacks with His truth.

READY

I love the saying, "Stay humble, hustle hard." When I originally considered this devotion, I thought it might be a good idea to split it into two devotions: one about "staying humble" and the other about "hustling hard." However, I realized that would be like separating peanut butter and jelly. The real magic is when you put the two together. Staying humble *while* hustling hard can lead us to become more like Christ.

Many teenagers I talk to think that humility is not bragging about yourself; however, the definition goes much deeper. Being humble is the act of serving others and placing them before yourself. Growing in humility takes time and requires dedication to your prayer life. A true understanding of our sin and God's grace brings us to our knees, and that is where we find humility. The Bible says that apart from Him, we can do nothing (John 15:5) because He has already done everything (John 16:33). Developing humility is a life-long process, so don't get discouraged if growth in this area seems slow – baby steps can produce dramatic changes in your relationship with the Lord and others.

Humbling ourselves before God will generate a spirit of reverence and gratitude that leads us to passionately serve Him and others. It is in this service that we must hustle hard. Though only God can do the miraculous work of transforming our minds (Romans 12:2), this does not mean we can just sit back and relax. God handles the work of salvation, but our part in

hustling hard is obedience. He will open our
hearts and minds to new experiences, some of which may be difficult.
Jesus never promised that following Him would be easy. We must
hustle hard in service to the King.

I learned the value of "staying humble, hustling hard" when my
family decided to go backpacking in Virginia on Thanksgiving Day.
We made this trip to celebrate both of my brothers' thirteenth birthdays.
Since becoming a teenager is a big deal, we wanted to celebrate my
brothers in a fun way, and they decided they wanted to take the entire
family backpacking. This was a humbling trip because neither my

mom, my sister, nor I had a burning desire to sleep in the woods during the winter, carry a heavy backpack, or hike sixteen miles over the course of twenty-four hours. However, we had to humble ourselves and remember that the celebration was for the boys - not us. We also learned the value of hustling hard because hiking on rocky, uphill terrain, sleeping in freezing temperatures, eating dehydrated food, and going to the bathroom in the woods was a lot of hard work. In the end, it was worth it because of the family time together, the adventures, and the experience of trying something new. I am not going to lie though; I will probably not go backpacking in the winter again because the cold was miserably brutal!

SET

"Do nothing from selfish ambition or conceit, but in humility count others more significant than yourself. Let each of you not only look to your own interests, but also the interests of others."

Philippians 2:3-4

"Whatever you do, work heartily, as for the Lord and not for men."

Colossians 3:23

GROW

Humility and hustling hard not only transform you, they also transform others around you. People will notice something different about you, and that difference is Jesus! I challenge you this week to ask the Lord to bless you with baby steps of humility. Always keep your eyes open for what God is doing in your life and challenge yourself to use what God has given you to bless others. Write the names of those you could serve below and get busy hustling for the Lord!

READY

In our world today, there are many opportunities to make your *"one of a kind"* mark on the world. For example, we all know of names like Martin Luther King, Jr., Elvis Presley, Simone Biles, J.K. Rowling, Rosa Parks, and Walt Disney. Why are these names so widely known? Most people recognize these names because these individuals accomplished something that made a difference in the world. Martin Luther King, Jr. stood up for his belief that all people are equal and deserve the same rights. Amen! We know the others because of their musical talent, Olympic performances, excellent storytelling, civil rights activism, and creativity. Each one has brought the world great joy and improvement, but there is only one person who made the biggest difference. His name is Jesus. God calls us to follow Jesus's example and strive to make a positive impact for His kingdom.

One experience I will never forget is a school missions trip to an Indian Reservation in South Dakota. The acts of service we provided in South Dakota seemed very small; however, the work we did made a large impact. The trip was a wonderful experience and helped me gain a new perspective. I learned that making a difference is often not a function of how big or small your actions are but is rather based on your willingness to create change.

In order to leave our unique mark on the world, we must think about our actions. To make a difference, we must be different. The people I mentioned earlier are special and are

recognized for what made their lives unique. Think about how different Jesus was from the rest of the crowd. He was kind, humble, compassionate, loving, and gentle. We should strive to be the same. In an effort to serve others, we need to shift our focus toward other people. Being different is not easy. Jesus was not always praised for

His actions and words, and neither were the people I listed previously. Jesus was persecuted for His faith, and you might be challenged because of yours, too. Not everyone who makes a difference is praised all the time, but know that Christ will always bless you for your obedience. Christ must be our focus!

SET

"Do not be conformed to this world, but be transformed by the renewal of your mind, that by testing you may discern what is the will of God, what is good and acceptable and perfect." Romans 12:2

"And he said to them, 'Go into all the world and proclaim the gospel to the whole creation.'"

Mark 16:15

GROW

Make a difference by being different. Pray about how you can make a difference in someone else's life. Are there ways you can make a difference right now? Who is a person you admire? What makes this person different from others? Do you think this person has faced challenges in his or her life because of these differences? Write down any ideas you have in the space provided below.

READY

To kick off 2020, I went to the gym on New Year's Day to workout. While I was doing some push-ups, someone approached me and asked me if I wanted to do a core workout. I agreed and let this person lead me through the hardest core workout I have ever done. We did 5 sets of 20 burpees totaling 100 in all. I do not typically include burpees into my workouts, and I could not believe I was having such a hard time! In fact, I could barely move the next three days because of how sore I was.

Just like I worked hard at the gym, we need to work hard when we train ourselves spiritually, too. As Christians, it should be our goal to train to become more godly every day. There is a popular acrostic that is helpful to think about before you do or say anything: "What would Jesus do (WWJD)?" This phrase reminds us to act, speak, and think as Jesus would under all circumstances. First, acting like Jesus includes how we handle situations, how we communicate with others, and what we dedicate our time toward. God commands that we do all things in love. Whether we are working out an argument, hanging out with a friend, or playing basketball at school, we should do all things with the love of Christ. Second, we should aim to speak like Jesus. In James 3:6a, it states "And the tongue is a fire, a world of unrighteousness." We must watch our tongue and train it to proclaim what is godly. One thing that helps to tame the power of the tongue is God's word. The Bible is full of verses that remind us to speak in ways that glorify the Lord. My mom often tells me and my siblings, "It's

not only what you say, but how you say it." Our words can be used to hurt or help. Let's choose to help others because building people up in the truth of God's word exemplifies the love of Christ. Lastly, in His Word, Jesus tells us to think on things that please, glorify, and honor Him. When we think of godliness, our actions and words will flow from good thoughts. This does not come naturally for any of us; however, we should work toward thinking godly thoughts by remaining in communication with God and filling our spirits with His Word.

"Have nothing to do with irreverent, silly myths. Rather train yourself for godliness; for while bodily training is of some value, godliness is of value in every way, as it holds promise for the present life and also for the life to come."

1 Timothy 4:7-8

"Finally, brothers, whatever is true, whatever is honorable, whatever is just, whatever is pure, whatever is lovely, whatever is commendable, if there is any excellence, if there is anything worthy of praise, think about these things."

Philippians 4:8

GROW

These verses remind us to train ourselves to be godly in our actions, words, and thoughts. Through His Word, prayer, and practice, we can become more godly and further grow His Kingdom. This week, think of three personal examples of how you can act, speak, and think more like Jesus. Journal these thoughts and ideas so that you can refer to them when you need a reminder.

READY

When I was in the 5th grade, I used to worry A LOT! Before I would go to sleep at night, I would ask my mom, "Where are you going to be?" in case I needed her. I was always worried something was going to happen in the night, and I would need to know where she was. She would respond with something like, "I'll be in the kitchen." I would then ask, "Where are you going to be after that?" This pattern of "Where are you going to be, Mom?" continued each night until finally my mom told me it was time for bed. Now that I look back, the things I was worrying about were silly and didn't even matter! Most importantly though, God was able to handle all my worries.

To overcome worry, the first thing I decided to do was to give all my concerns to God. I prayed asking Him to calm my nerves and anxieties. Every night before I went to sleep, I prayed, and it helped relax my spirit. If you continue praying to Him, you will be able to feel His presence and see how He is answering your prayers. God doesn't always work on our timing, but trust that He hears your prayers and will answer them according to His will and timing. It is important to keep in mind when praying that nothing is too big or too small for God to handle. Whether it is a struggle in a relationship, your grades in school, or your performance in an extra-curricular activity, God is able, and IF you are willing to give the situation to Him, He will handle it for you. Jesus is your best friend, and you can depend on Him to help you with

anything – whether it is big or small. God says He
holds the entire world in His hands, which means He has got you
too. Knowing that we are in His hands, we must let go of our fears,
worries, and weaknesses and give them to the Lord in prayer. He will
take care of you; trust in Him. You are His child, and He will guard
and protect you always and forever.

"Therefore, I tell you, do not be anxious about your life, what you will eat or what you will drink, nor about your body, what you will put on. Is not life more than food, and the body more than clothing? Look at the birds of the air: they neither sow nor reap nor gather into barns, and yet your heavenly Father feeds them. Are you not of more value than they? And which of you by being anxious can add a single hour to his span of life? And why are you anxious about clothing? Consider the lilies of the field, how they grow: they neither toil nor spin, yet I tell you, even Solomon in all his glory was not arrayed like one of these."

Matthew 6:25-29

"Do not be anxious about anything, but in everything by prayer and supplication with thanksgiving let your requests be made known to God. And the peace of God, which surpasses all understanding, will guard your hearts and your minds in Christ Jesus."

Philippians 4:6-7

GROW

These verses helped me a lot through the times I worried, and I still enjoy reading them today. They serve as a reminder for how much God loves us. God's word is alive and active! Besides turning to scripture, spend time alone with God in prayer to share your worries. This week, write down any worries that are troubling you. Pray, trusting God with each situation. Do not be afraid to call upon His name; that is what He is here for.

READY

Do you want to hear the sweetest story ever?

My parents met in the 5th grade. They were friends throughout middle school; however, they did not begin dating until their senior year of high school. They continued dating in college and were married a month after they graduated. Even though my parents have known each other since they were 11 years old, they were not each other's first love. Before my parents fell in love with each other, they fell in love with Christ. Loving God before you commit to loving anyone else is so important! We cannot properly love others if we have not received the perfect love Christ graciously pours over us. In Matthew 22, God provides the two greatest commandments. God says "Love the Lord your God with all your heart and with all your soul and with all your mind. This is the great and first commandment." Next, He declares "love your neighbor as yourself." The first commandment is listed before the second for an important reason. Before we can love anyone else correctly, we must love God.

The desire to form a relationship with someone of the opposite gender is natural and has existed from the beginning of time. Let's reflect on the story of the first couple to have ever lived: Adam and Eve. First, God created Adam and saw his need for companionship. Then, to create a partner for Adam, God literally formed woman by pulling one of Adam's ribs out from his body. We see through Adam and Eve that men and women depend on each other and receive love from one another. However, if men and women are not dependent on God's love

first, relationships can be destructive. Adam and Eve abandoned their love for the Lord by eating from the tree of the knowledge of good and evil. They broke the one and only rule God gave them, and God punished them. Adam and Eve believed the fruit from the tree of the knowledge of good and evil would offer them something greater than God's love. However, there is absolutely *nothing* greater than God's love. For any relationship to thrive, God must be our first love!

"But seek first the kingdom of God and his righteousness, and all these things will be added to you."

Matthew 6:33

"And he said to him, "You shall love the Lord your God with all your heart and with all your soul and with all your mind. This is the great and first commandment. And a second is like it: You shall love your neighbor as yourself. On these two commandments depend all the Law and the Prophets."

Matthew 22:37-40

GROW

I am eighteen years old, and while I have never dated, my life is full of relationships with my family and friends. I am especially thankful that during my high school years I have solidified God as my first love and my most important personal relationship. Remind yourself this week that before you love others, you must solidify your love for Christ. Read the story of Adam and Eve in Genesis 2 and 3. Pay careful attention to how God designed Adam and Eve and notice how their story greatly changes when their love for God is neglected. Also, think about the relationships God has placed in your life. Is God your first love? Please journal your thoughts in the space provided below.

READY

Distractions are everywhere in our world. One distraction in particular is a device that started out as a large object hung on the wall with a cord attached, and now, it is much smaller, quite efficient, and extremely popular. If you have not guessed it already, the object I am referring to is a cell phone. The phone's ability to call, text, and download apps makes it a powerful tool. The efficiency of communication has skyrocketed due to devices like phones; however, they can also harm our relationship with Christ IF we let them. Psychologists around the world have been studying the effects of phone usage on the human mind. They have found that phones distract people from doing homework, job activities, and chores. More importantly, as Christians, phones can easily distract us from spending time with Jesus. Before I go any further, I want to be clear: I am not trying to say you should not have a phone. I have a phone, and I think it is a great tool when used properly. However, our society has become obsessed with technology, causing a loss of focus on other areas of our lives.

As Christians, we should set an example of how to use our phones correctly. Many people today never separate themselves from their phones; however, it is very important to unplug! My parents made a rule that my sister and I must charge our phones downstairs at night. Your parents may have similar rules, and you may not enjoy them, but know that unplugging produces amazing results. Your parents make rules to protect

you, not to annoy, frustrate, or harm you. If your parents do not make rules for you, I suggest that you make some rules for yourself. Keeping my phone downstairs at night means I wake up without it sitting right next to me. Instead of waking up to check my phone, I get ready for the day and have my devotion. When you are meeting with God, it helps to put all distractions away. God tells us to go to a quiet place to dwell in His presence (Matthew 6:6). When you are talking with God, your phone needs to be put away and silenced, because what God tells you is far more meaningful than any text message, phone call, or notification you could ever receive. Phones often distract us from having quiet times with the Lord. This makes me so sad for our generation! We need time with the Lord. If you put away your phone for ten minutes each day to have a quiet time, you will begin to see life-changing outcomes.

Phones tend to distract us from others' physical presence around us, too. We may be communicating with other people online, but God created His people for *intimate* relationships. My pastor always says *"into me you see"* when he refers to *intimacy* because it serves as a reminder that to view people's hearts, we must be willing to communicate face to face. I challenge you to consider using your phone more responsibly and encourage others to do the same. Do not let those notifications stand in the way of your relationship with the Lord, your family, or your friends!

SET

"But when you pray, go into your room and shut the door and pray to your Father who is in secret. And your Father who sees in secret will reward you."

Matthew 6:6

GROW

Are you addicted to your phone? Try putting it down for extended periods and walking away. My guess is that your friendships will deepen, your stress levels will decrease, and your time with the Lord will become more meaningful. If your phone has the screen time feature, use it to record the time you spend on your phone. Do your best to decrease that number each day. Use the space below to record the amount of time you spend away from your phone each day this week. What activities did you do with this "new-found" time?

READY

During the COVID-19 pandemic, my family and I developed some new, fun traditions. Our first tradition began at the start of quarantine. My family decided to commit to having family devotions each night. Each person in our family prepared his or her devotion and shared it with everyone else on their assigned day of the week. Because we have six people in our family and not seven, we saved Sundays for church. This idea originated from my mom, and at first, I was hesitant because I was not sure if my family would truly stick to this weekly plan; however, it worked! Having devotions allowed each of us to learn more about each other, but more importantly, we were able to learn more about Christ. Our family devotional time concluded with prayer. The power of praying with others is absolutely astounding!

Also, during quarantine, my mom, my sister, and I delivered donuts (AKA: donut drops) to our four-year-old friends we serve at church. All three of us have been serving in the kid's ministry for two years. We are blessed to know several of the kids and their families very well; however, during the pandemic, we were not able to see them due to church being online. As a way of letting the kids know we missed them, we dropped off donuts at their homes and colored their driveways with chalk. It was so much fun and super simple, but hopefully this made a positive impact on the kids and their families. Each member of my family agreed to work toward encouraging others on a more intentional level. Whether you decide to make a donut

drop for a friend, send a kind text, or mail
a note, the little things in life usually make big impacts!

Another tradition my family decided to pursue during the pandemic
was letter writing. Even though it seems to be a lost art, letter writing
is very powerful and encourages people in positive ways. I decided to

write notes to my teachers, friends, and every student in my grade. It was such a wonderful experience. Seeing the ways in which a simple note can bless someone continues to bring joy to my heart! Writing letters and receiving mail from friends are two things that I greatly value because I know the time and effort involved.

These new traditions my family developed during quarantine will hopefully encourage you. It is never too late to change your habits and start new traditions. God reminded me through the pandemic, though He never changes, He desires to see our hearts change. Allow God to transform your heart and the way you live! Making habits and traditions to bless others helps to spread the love of Christ to our neighbors.

SET

"And I will give you a new heart, and a new spirit I will put within you. And I will remove the heart of stone from your flesh and give you a heart of flesh."

Ezekiel 36:26

GROW

This week start a new tradition. Ask the Lord to give you the strength to accomplish this and hold yourself accountable by writing it below.

READY

The picture in this devotion reminds me of a minor catastrophe. It was taken right after a shelf in my closet collapsed. Everything was a mess, which for an organized girl like me was a bit stressful! It was difficult to clean up and reorganize; however, the lesson I learned from my closet catastrophe was worth it. The items we own do not define us and are not important. If we build our lives on our earthly belongings, our spiritual foundation will eventually crumble. The shelf in my closet was not securely fixed to the wall. It was attached merely to the sheetrock and not anchored to the studs. If we anchor our lives on the wrong things, they will fall like the shelf in my closet. However, if we put our trust in Christ and allow Him to be our foundation, we will be able to stand firm.

There is always someone or something telling us to purchase the newest technology, trendiest clothing, nicest footwear, or coolest cars. Society makes us feel as though we must have all these things in order to be accepted. Advertisements, commercials, and even friends and family members can encourage us, indirectly or directly, to purchase these items. Sometimes, we crave items not for their intrinsic value but just because they are the next "big thing." This is not always negative; however, I do believe that the desire for earthly possessions can drive us away from the simple truth: All we really need in our lives is Christ.

I once heard someone say that "having stuff is not bad as long

as you own the stuff, and it does not own you." Matthew 19:16-24 tells the story of a rich young ruler who struggled with this principle. The young ruler questioned Jesus on how to receive eternal life. He proudly stated that he had kept all the Ten Commandments. Yet, Jesus challenged him to give up his possessions and follow him to receive eternal treasure. The rich young ruler left disheartened. He chose to hold on tightly to his earthly possessions, and therefore he was unable to receive the blessings Jesus offered. To be clear, wealth and possessions are not bad things. I have seen people use the riches and blessings that God has bestowed on them to bless others and further His kingdom. The trouble comes when we use these gifts from God to replace Him or when we pursue them instead of Him. Jesus knows the struggle that our earthly possessions can present. He warns of this in Matthew 19:24. The challenge for us is: Will we be like the rich, young ruler and go home disappointed, or will we lay down our possessions in order to receive God's blessings?

SET

"Do not lay up for yourselves treasures on earth, where moth and rust destroy and where thieves break in and steal, but lay up for yourselves treasures in heaven, where neither moth nor rust destroys and where thieves do not break in and steal. For where your treasure is, there your heart will be also."

Matthew 6:19-21

"Again I tell you, it is easier for a camel to go through the eye of a needle than for a rich person to enter the kingdom of God."

Matthew 19:24

GROW

You might be thinking that this does not apply to you as you are not rich. However, the average monthly income in my brother's home country of the Democratic Republic of the Congo is less than $50 per month. Most teenagers make more than that in one night as a babysitter! By almost any measure, most Americans are indeed "rich." I challenge you this week to think about your favorite earthly possessions. List your top five below. Journal how hard it might be to give those up.

READY

Recently, my family hosted a graduation party for a family friend. Along with the catered dinner, there were several delicious desserts. Everyone knows that a party is not complete without desserts! We had Oreo Cheesecake, homemade cookies, and a vanilla sheet cake with buttercream frosting. Instead of having one of these wonderful desserts, I decided to be healthy and eat fruit. My mom had bought a huge pineapple, and it was probably one of the best I had ever tasted. Pineapple has always been a special treat, so I chose to eat more than usual. After the party was over, I began itching like crazy. I assumed it must have been due to mosquito bites. I went to bed feeling itchy, but I wasn't worried. It was just a few bug bites. However, the next morning, I began to feel itchy again on the back of my legs. As I kept scratching, I looked down to find my legs were covered in giant, red welts! I suddenly realized that my so-called bug bites were not bug bites! Instead, I was having an allergic reaction from eating too much pineapple at the party. At first, I did not regret eating the yummy pineapple, but after being itchy for almost seventy-two hours, I decided that it would be best if I stayed away from pineapple for the rest of my life!

I learned two lessons from this experience. First, as Adam and Eve learned in the garden, not all things that look or taste great are good for you. The pineapple I consumed started as a delicious treat. This is the same with many sins. They seem pleasurable initially, but the consequences of our sin can be downright painful! I began enjoying the pineapple because it

was delicious, and I continued to go back for more. However, my opinion of pineapple changed after the painful allergic reaction. Second, I quickly learned that too much of anything can be harmful. I probably ate thirty pieces. People can consume too much of video games, television, social media, sweet treats, and possessions. The only thing that you cannot have too much of is Jesus! Unlike the previous list of items, Jesus will never cause a negative effect on your life. We always benefit from time spent with Him. Consume more of Christ! You will begin to find that when you pursue Jesus more, He will pursue you more, too!

"If you have found honey, eat only enough for you, lest you have your fill of it and vomit it."

Proverbs 25:16

"So when the woman saw that the tree was good for food, and that it was a delight to the eyes, and that the tree was to be desired to make one wise, she took of its fruit and ate, and she also gave some to her husband who was with her, and he ate. Then the eyes of both were opened, and they knew they were naked. And they sewed fig leaves together and made themselves loincloths."

Genesis 3:6-7

"Seek the Lord and his strength; seek his presence continually!"

1 Chronicles 16:11

GROW

Write down anything you are consuming in excess – food, screen time, shopping, etc. Commit to consuming less of those things and more of Jesus! You will learn more of His goodness if you consume more of Him each day.

READY

Have your parents ever made you do something you really did not want to do? I remember in the middle of my first grade year, I moved across the country from cold, northern Michigan to hot, southern Texas. These two places are quite different, and I was very nervous, especially about my new school. On my first day at my new school in Friendswood, Texas, I remember walking into the building seeing nothing but unfamiliar faces. During morning drop off, students were gathered in the lunchroom until school started. Because it was my very first day, my parents walked me inside. We found my designated class spot in the lunchroom. The cafeteria was loud, and I was surrounded by kids who were all bigger than me. I did not want to stay, and I begged my parents not to leave me at school with all these children I did not know. My mom and dad reassured me that everything was going to be just fine, but my teacher was not particularly loving and was not what you would picture as an ideal first grade teacher. Even though I was not fully convinced right away, my parents did make me feel better. Ultimately, they knew I had to stay at school that day because if I did not adjust quickly, it would make things more difficult later.

We have all been under our parents' authority. We have been places because we had to be, not because we wanted to be. Mike Haman, the pastor at our previous church in Baton Rouge, Louisiana, said "I am not here because I have to be, I am here because I want to be," every Sunday before he started

to preach. He would tell us that coming to church is a choice that we make. Even though people come to church, some still feel like it is required. Church is not required to achieve salvation; however, as we grow with Christ, church should become something we enjoy. Church is a joyful place where people worship the Lord, learn His word, fellowship with other believers, and experience His presence! Matthew 18:20 says, "When two or more are gathered in my name, I am there." My current pastor, Derwin Gray, says that church is not a place. Instead, it is the gathering of God's people to worship the Lord.

Unfortunately, many people dislike church because they think it is boring. Church can seem this way; however, zoning out is not the solution. Instead, listen carefully to what your pastor says and think about how it could apply to your life. If you focus on the fact that the church is about God, worshiping Him, and being in His presence rather than focusing on yourself or your feelings, church becomes about Him and not about you! Sometimes people do not attend church because they do not have any friends there. Anyone who is a follower of Christ can be your friend! Be willing to meet new people and get involved where you can. Talk to others before or after service, invite them to lunch, or simply shake their hand and ask them how they are doing. Serving at church is another way you can get to know others. Whether it is the children's program, the welcoming committee, the media ministry, the worship team, or small groups, there are many ways you can get involved. God does not desire for church to feel like something we have to do. He wants us to enjoy church and cherish being in His presence with fellow believers.

SET

"Now you are Christ's body, and individually members of it."

1 Corinthians 12:27

GROW

I challenge you to go to church with a fresh, new attitude. Focus during the sermon and take some notes this week at church in the space provided below. Stay attentive and seek to learn something new each Sunday! List ways you feel God could use you to serve your church.

READY

My Honduras mission trip was life-changing. One of my favorite parts of the trip was being with the Honduran children. We visited their schools, and I will never forget their joy and gratitude. Before we visited each school, we packed simple bags for each child with two coloring sheets (not a coloring book, but simply two pages torn out of a coloring book), two crayons, a pencil, toothpaste, a toothbrush, and six pieces of candy. Most Americans could easily find these items lying around the house, but these gifts were rare treasures to the Honduran children. Out of all the items in this bag, the pencil brought the loudest cheers from the children. It was not a glamorous pencil with pom poms on top, sparkles, or bright designs. It was just a simple yellow #2 pencil. Their excitement caused me to reflect on how many pencils I have in my house. We easily have more than two hundred! Imagine how excited these children would be if instead of one pencil they received two hundred! Oh, how we take so much for granted! It is so easy to forget how blessed and privileged we are. Even the simple act of flushing the toilet is something they cannot do in Honduras. Because their sewage system is very basic, the Hondurans are not allowed to flush their toilet paper. This was a reminder for me to thank God for even the small blessings in my life.

While I was in Central America, I thought constantly about the unfairness of my world compared to theirs. The people there did not do anything to deserve their poor living conditions,

and I did not do anything to deserve my privileged conditions. This realization brought about a sense of humility. The only reason I am blessed is so that I can bless others through what Jesus has given me. My abundance can meet someone else's need. We should always look for opportunities to bless others, even if it is simple. Often it is the simple things that make the biggest difference. God has equipped all of us to share our blessings with others, and I encourage you to do so with a happy, grateful heart.

SET

"Remember this: Whoever sows sparingly will also reap sparingly, and whoever sows generously will also reap generously. Each of you should give what you have decided in your heart to give, not reluctantly or under compulsion, for God loves a cheerful giver."

2 Corinthians 9:6-7

GROW

Ask God to provide opportunities for you to be generous to others. Sometimes, God will place an idea or person on your heart. Wherever God leads you to be generous, act quickly. Do not miss an opportunity to share with others! Write down a way in which you can bless others this week. For example, you could clean out your closet and donate clothes, toys, or shoes that you do not use or need anymore. Pray that God will show you a use for your unneeded items. God may place the name of a friend or family member on your heart. You might not know what their needs are, but God does!

READY

My sister, Mary Claire, is an incredible dancer. She dances competitively and has been tapping her toes since she was three years old. I love watching her dance because she exudes true joy as she performs. Her ability to dance is a God-given gift. I danced with my sister until I was in the eighth grade. At that time, I realized that dancing was not the calling God had placed in my life. I enjoyed dancing, and it was very special to me because I took lessons and performed in recitals with my sister, but I felt God telling me that I was called to something other than dancing.

The Bible mentions dancing for the Lord multiple times, implying that God deserves glory, and we are the ones to pour out our praise to Him. My sister praises the Lord by using her gift of dancing. When I watch my sister dance, I see grace in her movements, a gentle smile on her face, and a steady rhythm maintained throughout each step. She glides to the music and every step she takes is graceful. Like Mary Claire, we are encouraged to dance, too! Not all of us are competitive dancers like my sister; however, we can still praise God through dance. Mary Claire's dance moves match her song choice and the style of her routines. Our dance moves should align with the rhythm of God's grace, which is poured out to us every day.

Studies have shown that dancing helps people connect and communicate with others. I experienced this on my mission trip to Honduras. Because most of us could not speak very

"Let them praise His name with dancing."
Psalm 149:3

much Spanish, we decided
to dance with the kids, teens,
and adults. At each school we
visited, a giant dance party
broke out! We danced to fun,
Spanish songs, and everyone
loved it! I enjoyed dancing
because it reminded me that

communication takes on many forms and does not always require words. Dancing is something that most of us can do, and the best part is that it has the potential to unite people. We dance because Jesus loves us. We dance because His truth sets us free. We dance to unite with others and the Lord.

SET

"You have turned for me my mourning into dancing; you have loosed my sackcloth and clothed me with gladness."

Psalm 30:11

"Let them praise His name with dancing."

Psalm 149:3a

"Praise him with tambourine and dance; praise him with strings and pipe!"

Psalm 150:4

GROW

Dancing is one of many ways we can worship God. I love to dance! My mom loves dancing, too, but prefers a routine (5,6,7,8 approach!) due to her cheerleading days. My dad has no rhythm and prefers not to dance because it makes him uncomfortable. His skills and talents lie elsewhere, as in math and science. My brothers love to dance, and I wish you could witness their style, because it is quite hilarious to say the least. Do you like to dance? Even if not, give it a try this week. Turn on your favorite worship song and dance your heart out, like no one is watching. If you need some inspiration, check out Matt Harding in his 2016 YouTube video. Journal about your dance experience in the space below.

READY

Let's face it, we all make mistakes - lots of them! While no one likes to dwell on his or her shortcomings, mistakes offer an invitation to learn. Reflecting on our mistakes can be crucial to helping us become stronger Christians. It is a sign of spiritual maturity when we can realize what we have done wrong and properly address it.

Since sin affects us all, it is important that we understand how to handle it. First, we must recognize and admit that we have done something wrong. We need to take responsibility for the sin we have committed. Next, we should humbly ask God for His forgiveness. Without this step, our sin remains a weight that burdens us. God is the only one who can free us from this burden. After completely surrendering the sin to God, we should then reflect on our sin and look to Him for wisdom. What should we do to improve? How should we have handled the situation in a more Christ-like way? What should/shouldn't we have done? Did we hurt someone? Did we fail to love others? Did we give into Satan and his temptations? Were we following the wrong crowd? Through the Holy Spirit and the Bible, God can provide us answers to these questions. Lastly, it is crucial to make amends with those affected by our sin. Apologizing and asking for forgiveness is never easy, but it will make life so much easier once you do it. You will feel a burden lifted off your chest! Asking for forgiveness from both God and others is very important. No one likes to admit when he or she has done something wrong. Owning your words and actions requires great strength, but it results in true freedom.

150

In similar fashion, we must also know how to handle others' sin. Our job here is very simple. We are called to forgive. I have three siblings, and we sometimes drive each other crazy. That is just what siblings do! If you have siblings, you can probably relate. We might say words we wish we could take back or do things we wish we could undo. When I was little and had conflicts with my siblings, my mom used to make us hug one another or hold hands until we could genuinely say "I am sorry" to the other person. Can you imagine? We would start off frustrated with one another, unwilling to even look at each other. By the end of our hug session, we were laughing hysterically. My mom also resolved sibling conflicts by requiring us to give the other person a compliment. I used to wonder why she encouraged us to do this, but now, it makes sense. It is hard to dwell on the negative while you are giving compliments! When you forgive others, you must move past the mistake and see them as God would. God loves us in spite our mistakes; therefore, we should love others in spite of theirs.

SET

"If we claim to be without sin, we deceive ourselves and the truth is not in us. If we confess our sins, he is faithful and just and will forgive us our sins and purify us from all unrighteousness."

1 John 1:8-9

"And if he sins against you seven times in the day, and turns to you seven times, saying, 'I repent,' you must forgive him."

Luke 17:4

GROW

Do you owe someone an apology? If so, write out what you might say to this person and make amends this week. Remember to include these three points in your apology.

#1 Own up

#2 Reflect

#3 Apologize

READY

A good friend of mine encouraged me to be "comfortable in the uncomfortable." This simple yet powerful statement became a personal challenge for me during my high school years. As soon as we begin our walk with Christ, God may start calling us to do things that will take us out of our comfort zone. We tend to think that our comfort zone is our permanent home – a place where we can be safe and relax. However, we only have one permanent home, and God is calling us closer to it each day. When God calls us to do something hard or unexpected, it can make us feel extremely uncomfortable, nervous, or fearful. Yet, we can confidently and faithfully step into that calling knowing He will help us grow, teach us beautiful life-long lessons, and draw us closer to our real home.

When I was in the eighth grade, I felt God challenging me to do something that made me quite uncomfortable. The girls in my grade were all very sweet, but formed separate friend groups, as do most girls at school. God challenged me to sit with another group of girls at lunch. This was so hard for me, and I just could not muster up the courage to do it! I regret not obeying the Lord in this situation because I now realize all the positive outcomes that might have developed. I missed an opportunity to become better friends with the girls I usually did not talk to as much, and I would have gained more confidence through the process.

My sister, Mary Claire, stepped out of her comfort zone when
she decided to switch schools the summer before her sophomore
year. During the end of her freshman year, at the same time of the
COVID-19 pandemic, she decided to apply to the dance program

at a school called CATA (Central Academy of Technology and Arts). Both Covenant Day and CATA are wonderful schools; however, their environments differ. Covenant Day is a Christian, private school and CATA is a public magnet-based high school. Mary Claire enjoyed Covenant Day and was comfortable there because she was surrounded by people who shared the same beliefs; however, her comfort did not stop her from obeying God's call on her life. She knew that the Lord was leading her to CATA, and she obeyed Him with confidence.

God is bigger than your fear! He desires to use you in mighty ways, but you must be willing to be uncomfortable! Most likely, being out of your comfort zone will feel different and intimidating. Embrace the fact that taking a leap of faith will help you to improve in areas where you are weak and to grow deeper in your faith. God has great things to share with you… so step up for God and step out in faith.

SET

"Have I not commanded you? Be strong and courageous. Do not be frightened, and do not be dismayed, for the Lord your God is with you wherever you go."

Joshua 1:9

GROW

Is God challenging you to do something that feels uncomfortable? My pastor, Dr. Derwin Gray, uses the word "Godfidence" to describe confidence in God's abilities rather than our own. Write a prayer below seeking Godfidence, to face this uncomfortable challenge that God has placed in your life.

READY

My sister loves to remind my brother that she saved his life when he fell in our pool at the age of two. As soon as my sister heard the splash, she bolted inside to alert my mom. In a panic, Mom ran outside and pulled him from the pool. Although my sister did not perform the rescue, her role was crucial. Without her, my mom would not have known that my brother was in danger, and he would have drowned.

Whether it is a firefighter rescuing a cat, a lifeguard saving a drowning swimmer, or a friend standing up for a defenseless person, all rescue stories involve someone meeting another person's need in a moment of danger or distress. The Bible is full of these same types of tales. God rescued the Israelites when Pharaoh's army was chasing after them. He rescued Noah and his family from the 40 days and 40 nights of rain and flooding. He rescued Daniel from the lion's den. He rescued Shadrach, Meshach, and Abednego from the fiery furnace. Scripture tells us that God is a rescuer.

You have probably noticed that rescue stories typically emphasize the rescuer, not the person being rescued. It is the rescuer who is glorified and praised. This is most definitely true in the Bible. The Bible is written to praise the Great Rescuer, the One through whom we are all saved from our sins and given a new life. Let us rejoice in what our rescuer has done for us. We

are not hidden. there's never been a moment you were forgotten. You are hopeless, though you have been broken, your innocence stolen. I hear I whisper underneath your breath. I hear your SOS, your SOS. I will d out an army to find you in the middle of the darkest ght its true, i will rescue you. there is no distance that not be covered over and over. You're not defenseless. be your shelter ill be your armour. I hear you hisper underneath your breath, I hear your SOS, your SOS, will send rescue out an army to find in the dle of the darkest its true, I will cue. you, I will er stop marching to reach you in the middle of the hardest t its true, I will rescue you. I hear you whisper erneath your breath. I hear you whisper you have ing left. I will send out an army to find you in the le of the darkest night its true, I will rescue you. ll never stop marching to reach you in the middle of hardest fight its true I will rescue you. oh i will rescue you. ~mary

should give ALL honor, praise, and gratitude to
God. We do not deserve to be rescued; however, in His miraculous love, God CHOSE to do so. Aren't you glad God takes pleasure in saving His children?

"Even to your old age I am he, and to gray hairs I will carry you. I have made, and I will bear; I will carry and will save."

Isaiah 46:4

"The Lord will rescue me from every evil deed and bring me safely into his heavenly Kingdom. To him be the glory forever and ever. Amen."

2 Timothy 4:18

"The salvation of the righteous is from the Lord; he is their stronghold in the time of trouble."

Psalm 37:39

GROW

I encourage you to memorize one of the verses above that stands out to you. Also, this week listen to Lauren Daigle's song, "Rescue." You will feel blessed by the truth in her beautiful lyrics. What lyrics from the song speak to you? Write them below.

READY

Have you ever noticed that some people seem to find comfort in complaining? It is as if they feel better if they voice their dissatisfaction. Some repeated and common phrases are, "I am so tired," "Traffic is terrible," "School is boring," "Practice is so hard," "I don't understand my teacher," or "She is so annoying!" Why do we complain so often?

I am vertically challenged! Standing only 5'-2", I am shorter than most of my friends. It is something I have complained about more than once, especially when I need to reach that item on the top shelf of the pantry! Although I am short, God made me that way for a reason. There is nothing I can do to change my height (Doctors have told me numerous times that I will not grow any taller). However, I can rejoice in the way God designed me and ask my tall friends to grab the items on the shelves I cannot reach.

Despite the fact that we all do it, complaining does not provide any benefits! When we complain, we are simply listing the negative things in our lives. This changes nothing. In fact, it can actually make matters worse, as we often feel more frustrated or discouraged after complaining. You may have noticed that complaining is often contagious. Not only does it affect your attitude, but it can also bring down those around you. Nobody wants to be with a "Debbie-downer." To avoid complaining, we often need change our perspective. Abraham Lincoln once said, "We can complain because rose bushes have thorns, or rejoice because thorn bushes have roses." It is

all a matter of how you look at things. When you view things from a Christian perspective, you remember Jesus's tremendous sacrifice. He was persecuted and nailed to a rugged cross to die for us, and yet we are the ones complaining! In light of this great truth, all of our complaints seem silly and insignificant. He did not voice a single selfish complaint! In response, we should focus on the things we can control and make a difference where we can. If you want to see a difference, you have to BE the difference. You cannot control everything, but you can avoid complaining! Focus on the roses and not the thorns, and be grateful for the blessings in your life!

SET

"Do everything without complaining or arguing."

Philippians 2:14

"Give thanks in all circumstances; for this is the will of God in Christ Jesus for you."

1 Thessalonians 5:18

GROW

When we feel like complaining, we can look to God's word to remind us of His tremendous blessings. List at least five things you are thankful for in the space below so that you will remember the blessings God has given you. Complaining is a weapon Satan uses to steal your joy. Do not let Satan do that to you! Help yourself and others experience more happiness by vowing not to complain this week. When you get the urge to complain, refrain and change your perspective!

READY

If I were asked to describe the word "good," I would probably put it like this: "something or someone enjoyable." As an adjective, "good" can be defined as "to be desired or approved of, or having the qualities required for a particular role." Although this is the definition we are most familiar with, God's definition of "good" is completely different and surpasses all others. For certain, His is the most important. God's "good" can be described as anything that helps us become more like Him. One thing you may notice is that this definition of "good" is not as limited as the dictionary's. This one encompasses many more things.

From a Christian perspective, something can be defined as good if it will help us become more like Jesus. For example, injuries, sickness, change, and loss are all things we may think of as negative, but God uses these for our good. I realized this when my family moved from Georgia to North Carolina at the end of my 8th grade year. I have moved a total of nine times in my life, but this move was the hardest. When God called us to move to North Carolina, I thought, "Everything we could ever want or need is right here in Georgia." In other words, life was good…very good. Through this transition, I prayed to God asking for guidance, and I studied His Word more frequently. Looking back now, I could not imagine living anywhere else besides North Carolina. God has blessed my family here in ways I could have never dreamed. I have met people I cannot imagine not knowing and have been places I cannot imagine

not experiencing. Even the very book you are
reading would not have been written if I had not been challenged
with a senior project at my new school. Although I do miss Georgia,
God has blessed me tremendously in Charlotte, N.C. Despite my
worries and hesitations, God meant this move for "good" in my life.
It is a great reminder that God will use all things for good.

SET

"And we know that for those who love God all things work together for good, for those who are called according to his purpose."

Romans 8:28

"Not only that, but we rejoice in our sufferings, knowing that suffering produces endurance, endurance produces character, and character produces hope, and hope does not put us to shame, because God's love has been poured into our hearts through the Holy Spirit who has been given to us."

Romans 5:3-5

"As for you, you meant evil against me, but God meant it for good, to bring it about that many people should be kept alive as they are today."

Genesis 50:20

GROW

God controls every aspect of our lives, and He aims to work all things to the good of those who love Him. This week, I challenge you to memorize Romans 8:28. Write it down below and make a list of all the good God is doing in your life. These things may not appear good on the surface; however, I challenge you to look through a different lens and change your perspective to God's perspective. Write your thoughts in the space provided below. Also, listen to the song, "See a Victory" by Elevation Worship. The lyrics of this song remind us that "[God] takes what the enemy meant for evil and [God] turns it for good."

READY

In the fall of 2020, my friend answered a calling God laid on his heart to encourage fellowship by hosting worship nights every other Saturday. He gathered high school singers and musicians to lead students in worship. Even though this gathering was only held twice a month in his backyard, this time of fellowship enriched my life. During COVID-19, in-person fellowship opportunities were hard to find. Even with masks and social distancing, my friend's worship gatherings provided a wonderful way for me to fellowship with others through singing and prayer. One of the many aspects I love about my friend's worship nights was that he welcomed people from other schools. He knows the power of fellowship and desires to grow God's Kingdom through organizing and hosting these influential worship nights.

For believers, fellowship is necessary and can be powerful in helping us expand our faith. Jesus calls us to "gather together with one mind and spirit, thinking of others as better than ourselves" (Philippians 2:2-3). Often people are hesitant to branch out beyond their group of friends, preferring to stay in the security and comfort that their closest friends provide. However, for our fellowship to grow, we must set aside our fears and be intentional about expanding our circle to both believers and non-believers. While Jesus chose to invest heavily in his twelve disciples, He spent time with all types of people. He attended the wedding of a family friend, spent time at the

well with the Samaritan woman, wept with Martha and Mary over Lazarus' death, and had dinner at the home of Zacchaeus. Jesus is the King of Fellowship.

"So if there is any encouragement in Christ, any comfort from love, any participation in the Spirit, any affection and sympathy, complete my joy by being of the same mind, having the same love, being in full accord and of one mind."

Philippians 2:1-2

"I appeal to you, brothers, by the name of our Lord Jesus Christ, that all of you agree, and that there be no divisions among you, but that you be united in the same mind and the same judgment."

1 Corinthians 1:10

GROW

All of us should work towards embracing everyone, even if that means taking a risk or doing something uncomfortable. It is easy to hang out ("fellowship") with those who share the same interests, live in the same neighborhoods, and have the same backgrounds. However, God calls us to live in harmony with ALL people (Colossians 3:14). For this reason, we must be intentional about seeking out fellowship with each other. This week, I encourage you to reach out to at least two people whom God may be calling you to include in your fellowship circle. Reaching out could be as simple as a text message, a phone call, or writing a note. Pray for these two people God laid on your heart and expect your fellowship circle to expand.

READY

The summer before I started high school, I did something super crazy! We had just moved to Charlotte, and I decided to ride our skateboard down the driveway. Just to be clear, I am NOT a skateboarder. We had only lived in our new house for a week, and I was not familiar with everything yet. I did not realize our driveway was a long, gradual hill. As you can see, this story is already going downhill very fast! As I began riding down the driveway, it felt wonderful. The breeze was so refreshing, and it was awesome to cruise for a moment. The skateboard ride was going exactly as I had expected. However, as I kept riding, I gained more speed and momentum. I started to feel nervous because I was traveling so fast. Since I was a novice skateboarder, I did not know how to stop or slow down. My fear increased as I reached the end of our driveway. I had nowhere to go! In panic, I did the only thing I could think to do in the moment: I jumped off the skateboard to avoid hitting the garage and trees. A few seconds later, I heard my mom say, "Hannah Beth, are you okay?" I replied, "I'm good!" Then, I looked down and saw that I was covered in scrapes. I had seven large wounds: one on my right arm, my right hip, my chin, both hands, and both knees. What a doozie! I could not believe what just happened. In less than sixty seconds, I went from standing up confidently on the skateboard to tumbling across the concrete.

This skateboarding incident reminds me of how sin manifests itself in our lives. Just like my skateboard ride, sin is often a

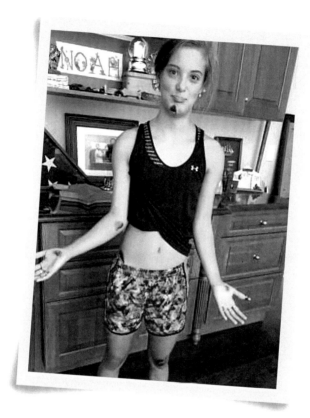

long, gradual downward spiral. My driveway
seemed relatively flat; however, I soon found out it was a steep
slope. I gained speed quickly on the skateboard and was unable to
stop. The same can be true with sin. Satan can deceive us, tricking
us into thinking "It is only a small sin." Yet, sin has powerful effects,
and one small sin can lead to bigger sins. If we are not careful, sins
accelerate and become abundant in our lives. Then we are unable to

stop and we fall. Sins never have a positive outcome, and neither did my skateboard ride. I was covered in scrapes before my freshman year at a new school! Not only was that painful on an emotional level, but it was very painful physically, too! I share this crazy story to remind you that sin can easily entangle us; however, it only has the power to trip us if we let it. With God's help, we can avoid sin and its dangerous affects. He will protect you from the downward spiral of sin by offering you His Word and His Spirit as guidance. With this valuable lesson learned, I do not intend to ever get back on a skateboard again!

SET

"Watch and pray that you may not enter into temptation. The spirit indeed is willing, but the flesh is weak."

Matthew 26:41

"Submit yourselves therefore to God. Resist the devil, and he will flee from you."

James 4:7

"So flee youthful passions and pursue righteousness, faith, love, and peace, along with those who call on the Lord from a pure heart."

2 Timothy 2:22

GROW

Keep away from sin by reading God's word and resting in His presence. With the Lord, you will not fall. He will keep you strong and help you resist temptation. Psalm 23:3 says, "He will lead you to the right path for His name's sake." Write a prayer below asking Him for His help and guidance.

READY

My family has moved several times, and there are specific things I miss about each place we have lived. I vividly remember the cold Michigan and Ohio winters and the heat in Texas and Georgia. We have lived in some larger cities like Baton Rouge, Louisiana and Charlotte, North Carolina. We have also lived in some places you have probably never heard of like Orangeburg, South Carolina and Ellerslie, Georgia. There are people, places, and things that I miss from all these states, and every now and then, I find myself reminiscing. I miss the houses I have lived in, the friends I have made, the country roads of Georgia, and the blueberry picking in Michigan. All these memories are precious and hold significant value in my heart. I have loved every place I have lived, and it is hard to leave what you love.

You certainly do not need to move as many times as I have to miss something. You may miss a lost loved one, a favorite family pet, life before your parents divorced. We may have to leave the things we love, but remember that the Lord will never leave us. He is with us wherever we go, and He has a purpose for every stage of our lives. God knows what He is doing! It is normal for us to question God's plan, but we need to keep our trust in Christ as we talk with Him. I encourage you to ask God questions, because that is a part of our walk with Him. His plan may seem unfair and confusing to you, but those feelings will fade as He begins to unveil the entire picture. When watching an artist draw, you may not at first be

able to tell what the picture will be, but keep watching, and it will make much more sense when you see the finished product. Sometimes, we feel as if we "need" what we miss, but all we truly need is the Lord. God is here to comfort you, to hold you, and to strengthen you when you need it most. His strengths are magnified in our weakness and loss.

At times, we can get consumed by focusing on the past, wishing things were the way they once were. This can cause us to miss the great things God has ahead of us. While wandering in the wilderness, the Israelites longed for their time in captivity as Egyptian slaves. They were too busy looking backward to see the Promised Land that God was delivering them into. It is okay to reflect back. In fact, the Bible is full of examples of people recalling their journey. However, do not let reminiscing cause you to miss what God is doing in and through you right now!

"Trust in him at all times, O people; pour out your heart before him; God is a refuge for us."

Psalm 62:8

"You keep him in perfect peace whose mind is stayed on you, because he trusts in you."

Isaiah 26:3

"That this is God, our God forever and ever. He will guide us forever."

Psalm 48:14

"God is our refuge and strength, a very present help in trouble."

Psalm 46:1

"And he made from one man every nation of mankind to live on earth, having determined allotted periods and the boundaries of their dwelling place."

Acts 17:26

GROW

Write down the people, places, or things you miss. As Psalm 62:8 says, pour out your heart to God! Let Him know how you are feeling, and you will eventually glean answers from God that will bring you peace and assurance.

READY

Each summer before school starts, my cross-country team retreats to a camp in the mountains called Ridge Haven. The retreat is four days long and is one of our hardest training sessions of the entire season. Despite the intense workouts, the trip is very enjoyable and serves as a great team-building experience. My most recent trip to Ridge Haven was quite memorable. For weeks, I had been recovering from an injury and had been unable to run. Just days before the trip, my doctor released me to start running again but urged me to take it slow. Because the camp was nestled in the mountains, the running trails were very hilly. My doctor advised me not to run the hills right away. Therefore, I was only able to run one mile a day, while the rest of my teammates were running eight miles a day! Instead, I mostly walked. As the team would line up to begin running, I would be the very last to go. I was always last, finishing behind everyone else. This was a new experience. As a runner, you never want to be last! Given my physical condition, I was the underdog of camp that year.

The Bible has a different view of those who are disadvantaged and facing tough odds. It offers hope to those left behind and encourages the underdogs. Joshua was able to lead the Israelites against the city of Jericho. His people could have easily been wiped out by the well-defended citizens of Jericho; yet, armed with only some trumpets and well-worn sandals, Joshua was able to bring down the massive walls of the city and claim

victory for God's people. Later in the Old
Testament, the young shepherd boy, David, faced off against the
giant Goliath. David was such an underdog that Goliath scoffed at
the idea that Israel had no one better to challenge him. Moments
later, Goliath was out for the count, and David was putting away his
slingshot. Even those who are last are blessed in the Bible. In the New

Testament, four friends of a paralytic man sought to bring him to Jesus for healing. Unfortunately, they were late to the party and could not enter the home where Jesus was teaching. Unwilling to give up, they found a means of lowering their friend through the roof. Despite being one of the last to arrive, their friend was blessed by Jesus with a healing! These stories demonstrate that with God's help, you can overcome tough odds.

At times in life, we may find ourselves the underdog, disadvantaged, or last. Know that God does his best work when we are at our weakest (2 Corinthians 12:9). Do not be discouraged because those who fall the farthest behind make the greatest comebacks with Christ.

SET

"But many who are first will be last, and the last first."

Mark 10:31

GROW

The Bible is full of inspirational stories to encourage us. This week read the full story of David (1 Samuel 17:1-25), Joshua (Joshua 6:1-27), and the paralytic (Luke 5:17-26). Draw a picture of your favorite story below.

READY

Have you ever had success walking in the dark?
I have tried, but unfortunately, it never turns out well. I end
up stubbing a toe, bumping my hip on the edge of the countertop,
or running into objects that I simply was not able to see.
Walking in the dark is very difficult, but thankfully, we have
electricity which gives us the option of turning on the lights.

Have you ever felt like you were walking in the dark spiritually?
I feel that way when I cannot see what God is doing in my
life or when I am unsure of where He is leading me. It is hard
for us when we cannot see the plans that lie ahead. The recent
COVID-19 pandemic has made our lives uncertain. Many
people are unsure of the future because the present is always
changing. During these rapidly changing moments, it can
become more difficult to see God and how He is leading us.
Although our uncertain circumstances may make us feel as
though we are walking in the dark, the Lord reminds us in
His word that His light provides vision. To see clearly, all we
need to do is reach for Him. Jesus is the light of the world.
Often, we are unable to see because we are not searching for
the light. We are told in Hebrews 13:8 that Jesus knows the
past, present, and the future. The Lord can see everything with
perfect clarity, so rely on His knowledge and wisdom. When
we are unsure of the future, we can ask God to reveal more of
Himself in our hearts, and we can trust that He will prepare us
for what our eyes cannot yet see.

One morning while I was praying, God proclaimed a simple, yet powerful truth to my spirit: "You are not going to be able to exit the darkness unless you are steadily reaching for the light." God sees everything and is the light that illuminates our path, so we should constantly be reaching for Him. Only His light can keep us from stumbling in the dark.

"Again, Jesus spoke to them, saying, "I am the light of the world. Whoever follows me will not walk in darkness but will have the light of life."

John 8:12

"For God, who said, "Let light shine out of darkness," has shone in our hearts to give the light of the knowledge of the glory of God in the face of Jesus Christ."

2 Corinthians 4:6

"So, Jesus said to them, "The light is among you for a little while longer. Walk while you have the light, lest darkness overtake you. The one who walks in the darkness does not know where he is going."

John 12:35

"The true light, which gives light to everyone, was coming into the world."

John 1:9

GROW

With your eyes closed, draw a picture of your bedroom. Make sure to include all your furniture and your favorite belongings. Now open your eyes and see how you did. Would your drawing be better with your eyes open? Likewise, God's light helps to make our lives clearer. This week I challenge you to focus on "steadily reaching for the light" by memorizing John 8:12.

READY

At the end of my Honduras mission trip, the leaders planned a debrief meeting so each person could share what God laid on their hearts during the trip. The debrief meeting turned into a much-needed unloading time for everyone, lasting approximately four hours. People shared their burdens and troubles openly. As each person shared, I was shocked to hear of the brokenness, not only from the people of Honduras, but also from the people right in front of me! There were heart-breaking stories of divorce, neglect, abuse, and depression. I realized that even the people who appear to live perfect lives are very broken, myself included. The debrief meeting was eye opening because it reminded me that people really are not that different. All people, despite living conditions, location, and ethnicity, experience the same human emotions.

Around my house, my dad is the fixer. He can repair most anything. Yet, when it comes to our personal lives, there are simply some things we cannot fix. God does not call us to solve every problem. Only He can do that. He instructs us to bear one another's burdens (Galatians 6:2). In our walk of faith, we all experience times of hardship and difficulty. During these times, God calls us to comfort each other. Sometimes the greatest act of support we can offer someone is listening. Similar to the mission trip debrief, people find comfort in sharing their burdens with those who genuinely care to listen. Like my dad, our tendency can be to attempt to fix others'

problems. While we may know how to solve their issue,
I've learned that "people don't care how much you know until they
know how much you care." So, what does it look like to bear one
another's burdens? It means that our hearts will break for the same
things that break God's heart. When someone we love experiences
pain or hurt, we should feel their pain and hurt. God calls us to sit
with others in their struggle, listening and offering comfort.

"Bear one another's burdens, and thereby fulfill the law of Christ."

Galatians 6:2

"Rejoice with those who rejoice, weep with those who weep."

Romans 12:15

"And let us consider how to stir up one another to love and good works, not neglecting to meet together, as is the habit of some, but encouraging one another, and all the more as you see the Day drawing near."

Hebrews 10:24-25

GROW

This week, listen to the classic worship song, "Hosanna," from Hillsong. The lyrics have profound truth. Fill in the blanks below. Who around you might be going through a struggle? Write down the names of at least three people you could comfort this week and ask God to give you the courage to follow through.

_____ my _____ for what

breaks yours. _____ *I am for your*

_____ *cause. As I* _____

from _____ *into eternity.*

READY

My brother, Muntu, is a great helper. This may sound like a small thing, but he truly is the best in our family at cleaning, especially sweeping and vacuuming our floors! He is also incredibly strong. Even though he is only thirteen, if you asked him to move the couch across the room, he could do it all by himself. Muntu definitely uses his God-given gifts to help others.

Helping others does not just involve what you do to help, it involves how you do it. Many people are willing to help, but do not have the right attitude. My parents and teachers have always told me "attitude is key." We must remember that helping others is not about us. We cannot allow our minds to be consumed with thoughts that focus on ourselves or what we will gain in return from helping others. We must put ourselves aside! Your heart must be in the right place when you commit to helping those around you. Change your mindset when you help somebody else. Do not focus on what is in it for you; instead, trust what God can do through you to help others.

We need to understand that we cannot help others if God does not help us first. In Ephesians 2:10, it says, "we are God's workmanship created in Christ Jesus for good works, which God prepared beforehand that we should walk in them." We have the privilege of being sons and daughters of God, which means we can ask God to give us the strength, patience, ability, and positive attitude to help others and do the works God has prepared for us. God has specifically gifted you with

talents that He intends for you to use to serve His people. Helping is no ordinary task; it is a high calling. Think about Jesus. The king of all the nations helped others! When the Holy Spirit calls you to help someone else, you should be honored. God knows that it is hard to help others, but He has gifted you with talents and abilities to share. Accept the calling of helping and use it to glorify God. He will bless you for helping others in their times of need and will change your heart tremendously! When you help others, you begin to see more of how the Lord has helped you along your journey.

"And the crowds asked him, "What then shall we do?" And he answered them, "Whoever has two tunics is to share with him who has none, and whoever has food is to do likewise."

Luke 3:10-11

"Do not neglect to do good and to share what you have, for such sacrifices are pleasing to God."

Hebrews 13:16

"Give to the one who begs from you, and do not refuse the one who would borrow from you."

Matthew 5:42

GROW

Help a friend, neighbor, or even a stranger with a JOYFUL attitude.
Start with one thing you can consistently do once a week. Write it
down and stick to it!

READY

My family loves to take long walks on the beach. On our last beach vacation, we decided to go for an extra long walk because it was so beautiful outside. As the walk progressed, we noticed dark clouds quickly approaching. We were more than a mile from our resort, so we decided it might be best to head back. We did not want to get caught in a storm! As we were power walking back, we all admired the beauty of the beach. The sun was still shining, and the water was crystal clear. The storm clouds were an interesting contrast to this beauty. It looked as if the dark clouds were rubbing right up against the blue water at the horizon. What an amazing sight!

Much like that image from the beach, light and darkness coexist spiritually also. Both are real and present in our world. They are polar opposites and yet share a connection in that one can be defined in terms of the other. Darkness is the absence of light. Without light, darkness envelops us and, in essence, blinds us. Thankfully, light always drives out darkness. Where there is light, darkness simply can not exist. Light is so powerful that even a little bit goes a long way. The human eye can see the flame of a candle from over one mile away!

The Bible tells us that Jesus is the Light. Only He has the power to drive out darkness. This is an important truth to remember because dark times in life will come: you may experience a hard breakup, you may suffer a season-ending injury, your closest friend may move away, your dad may lose his job, your sister may develop an illness, or you may be overcome with guilt or shame

from a past sin. When the storm clouds of life close in on you, don't power walk... run to the light. He can protect you and offer you shelter from the storm.

"The light shines in the darkness, and the darkness has not overcome it."

John 1:5

"Again Jesus spoke to them, saying, 'I am the light of the world. Whoever follows me will not walk in darkness, but will have the light of life."

John 8:12

"This is the message we have heard from him and proclaim to you, that God is light, and in him is no darkness at all. If we say we have fellowship with him while we walk in darkness, we lie and do not practice the truth. But if we walk in the light, as he is in the light, we have fellowship with one another, and the blood of Jesus his Son cleanses us from all sin."

1 John 1:5-7

GROW

Where is the darkness in your life? What hardships or difficulties are you facing? Write these things in the space below and illustrate your image of light coming through the darkness. Ask God to transform the darkness in your life to light. Know also that you can reflect God's light into the world. Just like that candle flame, the smallest glimmers of God's light in us can be seen from far away. God wants to use you to light up His kingdom. For encouragement, listen to the song "In Jesus Name" by Israel Houghton and New Breed. The lyrics of this song remind us that God is pushing back the darkness and has already overcome the world!

READY

My cross-country teammates and I encourage each other a lot! As we are racing or practicing, we often say to one another, "Ignite the glutes!" You might think that is the weirdest saying ever, but it helped unify our team by igniting a spark of encouragement to finish the race with all our might. The last half mile of the race is the hardest. At this point, our lungs are burning, and our muscles are tired. Life can sometimes feel this way, especially when we go through tough times. It is in these times that words of encouragement can be most powerful.

Together, we can encourage one another and build each other up. You have most likely heard the saying "teamwork makes the dream work." When we unite, it ignites sparks of positivity. My friends, family, coaches, and teachers have all encouraged me and helped me ignite the spark that produces determination and perseverance. By encouraging others, you not only help other people, but you also learn to become a better friend, sibling, teammate, and student. Bringing out the best in others also brings out the best in you! It may seem difficult at first, but by giving a genuine, thoughtful compliment, you are spreading seeds of God's love. He sees your hard work, and He will bless you for all you do to honor Him.

SET

"Therefore encourage one another and build up one another, just as you also are doing."

1 Thessalonians 5:11

"So then let us pursue what makes for peace and for mutual upbuilding."

Romans 14:19

"Two are better than one, because they have a good reward for their toil. For if they fall, one will lift up his fellow. But woe to him who is alone when he falls and has not another to lift him up! Again, if two lie together, they keep warm, but how can one keep warm alone? And though a man might prevail against one who is alone, two will withstand him—a threefold cord is not quickly broken."

Ecclesiastes 4:9-12

GROW

I challenge you to work towards being an encourager! Write down the names of at least five people you can encourage this week. God puts opportunities in our lives for a reason, so do not ignore them, accept them! Whether it is a family member, friend, classmate, coach, teacher, or a stranger, look for ways to encourage all people, just as Jesus does for us. One of my favorite ways to bless people is by writing notes. I sometimes mail my notes, but I also love to surprise people with a note in their locker, bookbag, or car. Letter writing seems to be a lost art, but I say we keep it alive! Who will you write an encouraging note to this week?

READY

Have you ever been to a place where there is trash everywhere you look? When I was in the beautiful country of Honduras on a mission trip, I saw an incredible amount of trash along the roads. While there, our group decided to clean up a few areas. We picked up trash in one of three locations. Some of the trash was directly in front of our eyes, other pieces were embedded in the ground, and some were beyond our reach behind fences or down steep hills.

All this trash reminded me of the sin in our lives. Have you ever noticed how we try to categorize our sins? We rationalize that "small" sins like lying or cheating are "better" than "big" sins like adultery or murder. Further, like the trash we picked up, we often classify our sins based on how hard we perceive it will be for God to clean it up. We see some sin as a quick clean up, while we consider other sins outside of God's forgiving reach. Unlike our efforts to compare and categorize our sin, God takes a simple, direct view.

It is all trash.

From God's perspective, it is all gross. It is all dirty. It is all just trash. But because of His mercy and love, God will forgive you for ALL sins, no matter how big or small. Jesus's death insured your forgiveness. By no means does this truth allow us to go on consciously sinning if we are committed to a relationship with Christ. However, it means that as we faithfully follow Him, He forgives us for the mistakes we make – obvious,

buried, or disregarded. So then what? Being sinful humans who will inevitably sin, what do we do after we have asked for forgiveness? My mom often reminds me and my siblings, "It's not about the mistake, but what you do with the mistake." Confession of our sin involves admitting to God that we have done wrong. This is key to God granting us forgiveness; however, we must also repent of the sin to avoid repeating it. Repentance means making a commitment to leave the sin behind and draw nearer to God. Trust in the power of Jesus's blood to wash away your sin, and rest in the promise that the Holy Spirit will help you repent.

SET

"In him we have redemption through his blood, the forgiveness of sins, in accordance with the riches of God's grace."

Ephesians 1:7

"If we confess our sins, he is faithful and just and will forgive us our sins and purify us from all unrighteousness."

1 John 1:9

"Repent therefore, and turn back, that your sins may be blotted out."

Acts 3:19

GROW

This week, I encourage you to pray asking God to reveal any sins you have buried in your heart. Ask Him for forgiveness and rest in knowing the wonderful truth that Jesus's blood was shed for you, so that your heart and soul could be cleansed. Draw a big heart and inside of it, list areas of your life that you need to surrender to the Lord. When you are done, get five small pieces of paper. On each piece, write one sin that you have been harboring in your heart. As you confess and show repentance for each sin, tear up the paper and throw it in the trash to symbolize God's forgiveness.

READY

God created the entire world for us, He sent His son to die for us, and He has characteristics unlike anyone else. His love is never ending. His faithfulness never ceases. We will always find hope in Him. God has done nothing but good things in our lives; therefore, He deserves some praise! We need to use the ten-string instruments God gave us - our hands - to show that we love Him.

One of my favorite opportunities to praise the Lord is attending Christian camps. Two that have really made an impact on my faith are Windy Gap, a Young Life camp I attend each year with my high school, and Sold Out Summer, a camp at a beach in Florida. The praise and worship at both camps is absolutely amazing! Another worship experience I will never forget occurred while I was on a mission trip at the Pine Ridge Reservation in South Dakota. Our group was leading the church service, and we began by singing worship songs with the members of the local church. The church on the Pine Ridge Reservation is very small, and few people attended this particular Sunday; however, the power of corporate worship remained evident as we all praised the Lord together. Similarly, when I traveled to Honduras on a mission trip, we attended a church service as well. The songs we sang were in Spanish, and my Spanish is not muy bueno; however, seeing the Hondurans pouring out praise for Jesus warmed my heart and reminded me how special worship is for all believers. Because we are all brothers and sisters in Christ, we have a common bond that overcomes language barriers and cultural differences. We are

one in Christ! I also love worshipping the Lord at my church, Transformation Church. Our worship team is very talented, and the way they lead us in singing praises to the Lord is life changing! Worship comes in many forms; however, the reason we worship remains the same. We are called to worship Him as a form of praise and to thank God for who He is and what He has done.

Not only are we called to worship God at church or at camp, living our lives for Christ is a form of worship, too! Through school, sports, and other activities, we are called to reflect God's glory. The most impactful way to worship God is through giving your life to Him. Jesus gave His life for you, a sinner, undeserving of grace and mercy, so you could give your life back to Him as a form of praise. When you give your life to Jesus, you are allowing Him to control every aspect of your life by surrendering everything to Him. Trusting Him with your life can be difficult; however, it is worth it! He who began a good work in you will not finish until it has reached completion (Philippians 1:6). If you live your life as a sacrifice to Him, Christ will provide everything you need. He may not do so in the way you imagined, but remember, no ear has heard, no eye has seen the great things God has prepared for those who love Him (1 Corinthians 2:9). Because God is so good all the time, praise Him with the ten-string instruments He blessed you with – your hands. Clap your hands for Jesus, show Him you love Him today, and be grateful for who He is and what He has done!

SET

"Oh, give thanks to the LORD, for he is good; for his steadfast love endures forever!"

1 Chronicles 16:34

"Clap your hands, all peoples! Shout to God with loud songs of joy!"

Psalm 47:1

GROW

Which of these two verses to the left is your favorite? Why is this your favorite? Journal your thoughts to these two questions below. Memorize your favorite verse on this list so that you can always remind yourself to praise the Lord for all He has done.

READY

Have you ever noticed how we are always looking for a perfect ending? Just like a good book or movie, all things eventually come to an end. Sometimes the ending is different than we expected. God shuts doors that we feel need to stay open and opens doors that we are not prepared to enter. We often envision the finish differently than God does. A lot of times, we question the ending. God does things in our lives that we do not understand, and we ask, "Is this really how it ends?" On the other hand, sometimes we are thankful for the way things end. Regardless of the outcome, remember God has a miraculous plan for you. He sees the full picture and always knows what is best for you. So, what you might think is the ending is really just the beginning.

As I wrapped up my eighth-grade year, my parents and I were in the midst of deciding where I would attend high school. The school I previously attended only went through 8th grade. As an eighth grader from a small, Christian school, the idea of a big, public school seemed a little scary. I applied for a scholarship for rising freshman at a non-Christian, private school. After anxiously waiting for feedback, we learned that the school offered five people a full scholarship, and I was sixth on the list. To know I was one spot away from earning this huge financial award was very disheartening; however, little did I know that when we moved to North Carolina, God opened another door after He closed that one. Now, I am attending a school very similar to the one I attended for middle

After two years, all 52 devotions are complete.

school, and I love it! I cannot imagine being anywhere else. I have
met wonderful friends and amazing teachers and have been involved
in my school's community in more ways than I thought were possible.
God knows exactly what you need and will provide for you at just the
right time and place. He loves you, and for every ending He creates,
there is an even bigger beginning waiting for you.

"For I am God, and there is no other; I am
God, and there is none like me, declaring
the end from the beginning and from
ancient times things not yet done, saying,
'My counsel shall stand, and I will
accomplish all my purpose.'"

Isaiah 46:9-10

"For I know the plans I have for you, declares
the Lord, plans for welfare and not for evil,
to give you a future and a hope."

Jeremiah 29:11

GROW

We can learn from God's ways and see things from a different perspective by studying His Word. God reveals a lot about Himself through the story of Moses and the Israelites. I have read the story of Moses many times; however, I am reminded of something different every time I read about how God used Moses and the Israelites to show His character, power, and love. Read the story of Moses in Exodus 2:11-15 and Exodus 14, and imagine what questions Moses must have had for God. While on the run after killing an Egyptian, Moses must have wondered how things would end. With the Egyptians behind him and the Red Sea in front of Him, did Moses wonder if this was the end? Journal below how Moses must have felt in these situations.

ALL MY THANKS...

First, I owe everything to my Lord and Savior, Jesus Christ. Without the Lord's guidance, strength, wisdom, love, and provision, I would have been unable to write this book. I am grateful for the ways in which Christ has led me along the journey of writing and for all the life-long lessons I have learned from Him during this process.

Mom – You introduced me to the wonderful idea of writing a devotional book for my senior project. Throughout the writing process, you have been by my side providing endless support and encouragement. You have given me wise advice and helpful guidance. Despite your busy days as a mom of four, you have found time to help me with edits. Your thoughts and insight are blessings I will treasure forever. Not only are you a fantastic mother, but you are also one of my best friends too.

Dad – You have supported me from the very beginning. No matter what God calls me to do, you are someone who will always be there to help me accomplish my goals. You have given amazing advice throughout the editing process. You use all the knowledge Christ has given you to help counsel me. I admire you, and I am beyond grateful God chose you to be my father.

Mary Claire – As my teenage sister, you provided incredible insight as I worked to write this book aimed at a teenage audience. I am so thankful for your constant encouragement and patience with this overwhelming project. Thank you for being my sister and my best friend.

Christy Murphy – You are SUNSHINE! Your beautiful spirit and spontaneity inspire me. You helped me tremendously by editing, providing comments, and giving suggestions throughout the entire writing process. Because of your amazing knowledge and experience, you were the first person I reached out to when I needed insight into the various steps of writing a book.

Becky Soileau – You have ALWAYS been a role model for me, and we are kindred spirits. You have loved, supported, and encouraged me. I am very grateful for your insight. Your thorough feedback made a huge difference in my writing.

Sue Mead – Thank you for helping me by reviewing my devotions with such attention to detail. You have such a sweet spirit and attitude. I am blessed to have you in my life, and I thank God for allowing us to be neighbors. I appreciate you so much!

Britton Goodling – Thank you for your tremendous help reviewing my devotions to ensure that they were a smooth, easy read. You are a blessing to all your students. I am grateful for our shared love and appreciation of words.

Christie Carey – Thank you for using your creative mind to design every detail of my devotional book. It was an absolute pleasure working with you and your God given gifts. This devotional book would not be the same if I had not received your help. So thankful for our "Shorter Girl" connection!

Lysa TerKeurst – I am tremendously grateful for the beautiful foreword you wrote for my devotional book. You are such an inspiration, and I am so thankful for your gift of writing and the way you use it to further God's kingdom.

Candance Salamone – You are one of the most beautiful spirits God ever created. Thank you for connecting me with Lysa TerKeurst. What an incredible blessing!

A huge thank you to my pastors who have modeled amazing leadership and faith. I would like to thank Mike and Rachel Haman, Jeff and Christy Murphy, and Dr. Derwin and Vicki Gray, for their support and encouragement. I am eternally blessed to have each one of you as spiritual leaders in my life. Your wisdom and inspiring sermons have poured words of life and love over me. I deeply appreciate each one of you and how you have helped strengthen the foundation of my faith. You are outstanding, and the world needs more people as kind-hearted as you!

To my dear friends, Vail Gaylord, Ellie Higgins, and Alexia Papanastasiou...thank you for being editors of my devotional book on our mountain retreat. It was such a refreshing experience to be together. I very thankful for the insight each of you provided. I love you all to pieces, and I am incredibly blessed to call you my friends.

Katie Spata – Thank you for helping me capture the vision for the cover of this devotional through your amazing photography skills. You are incredibly talented!

Heather Mills – Thank you for providing me the opportunity to work on this devotional book during the school year. I appreciate you and all you do!

Thank you to the faculty and leadership at The Dunham School (Baton Rouge, LA), St. Luke School (Columbus, GA), and Covenant Day School (Matthews, NC). Your nurturing and teaching have helped me grow tremendously in my relationship with Jesus.

My life is full of AMAZING people and I would like to thank all my friends and family members who have inspired me to write this book. The stories, memories, and personal touches involve you and how you have greatly impacted my life. Always remember I deeply love each one of you.

I would love to hear from you! If you can't find a carrier pigeon to drop me a note, you can reach me at readysetgrowdevo@gmail.com.

– Hannah Beth Brown

ABOUT THE AUTHOR

As her parents, we know Hannah Beth would never write about herself, so we begged for the job of writing the author description because other than her Heavenly Father, we know and love her best!

Hannah Beth Brown, also known as HB, is a high school senior at Covenant Day School in Matthews, NC. HB is the oldest of four children and loves to spend time with her family. Born in South Carolina, HB has lived in seven states and made many friends along the way. She is busy with countless school activities and babysitting jobs, but her favorite by far is pursuing the Lord and his plan for her life. Her love for Jesus has incredibly shaped her life. She has such a passion for loving and helping others through her gift of words and cheerful service. HB also has a love for running that is paired with an equal passion for health and nutrition. She is eagerly awaiting God to reveal His plan for college and her career paths.

One of her favorite verses is Philippians 4:5-7 *"Let everyone see that you are gentle and kind. Do not worry about anything, but pray and ask God for everything you need, always giving thanks. And God's peace, which is so great we can not understand it, will keep our hearts and minds in Christ Jesus."*

HB is also known as the "dish fairy and laundry fairy" at the Brown house, and so this note also serves as an ad for her replacement as she prepares to leave for college.